HEBREWS

LIVING BY FAITH

John Oakes & Robert Carrillo

HEBREWS: Living by Faith

Printed in the United States of America.

ISBN: 978-1-948450-86-7.

Unless otherwise indicated, all Scripture references are from the Holy Bible, New International Version, copyright ©1973, 1978, 1984, 2011 by Biblica, Inc. Used by permission. All rights reserved worldwide.

Cover design by Roy Apelsamy. Interior layout by Toney Mulhollan.

A special thanks to Amy Morgan for her editorial contributions.

Illumination Publishers titles may be purchased in bulk for classroom instruction, business, fund-raising, or sales promotional use. For information, please email paul.ipibooks@me.com.

Illumination Publishers cares deeply about using renewable resources and uses recycled paper whenever possible.

About the authors: John Oakes worked as a professor of chemistry and physics for over thirty years. In June 2018 he retired from full-time teaching and currently leads a church in Bakersfield, California. John became a Christian in 1978 while a graduate student at the University of Colorado. He earned his PhD in chemical physics there in 1984 and that same year married Jan. They have three children, Ben, Elizabeth, and Kathryn. John also serves as president of the Apologetics Research Society. He has taught on Christian topics in more than 80 countries and for 180 churches. Some of his other books include: *The Christian Story, Volumes I-III, Is There A God?, From Shadow to Reality, Reasons for Belief, Field Manual for Christian Apologetics* and *In Christ*. For more information about John's work, go to www.EvidenceForChristianity.org.

Robert Carrillo holds a master's degree in Divinity in 2012 from Pepperdine University. He was the CEO of HOPE worldwide from 2015 to 2019, where he has used his extensive biblical training, team building expertise and spiritual leadership in the nonprofit arena. He has led churches in Mexico, Florida, Jamaica, Puerto Rico, New Jersey, New York and San Diego, California. He and his wife, Michele, have been married since 1989 and have been blessed with three amazing children. Robert and Michele live and work with a church in Los Angeles.

Illumination Publishers International
www.ipibooks.com
6010 Pinecreek Ridge Court
Spring, Texas 77379-2513

LUMINATION PUBLISHERS

Contents

Acknowledgements

Special thanks to my wife Michele, who is my partner in the gospel, confidante, co- leader and soulmate.

Thank you John Oakes for pushing me to start writing. Thank you Sam Laing for instilling in me a passion for the word.

—Robert Carillo

Thanks to my good friend Robert Carrillo who is a mentor to me in the teaching and preaching of the gospel. Thanks also to my amazing wife Jan who follows me and supports me in my many adventures.

—John M. Oakes

Introduction

The book of Hebrews is truly one of God's great gifts to the Church. Beautifully composed, it is distinct from any of the letters or Gospels in the New Testament. In reality, it is neither a letter nor a gospel. If read aloud, as was originally intended by the author, it flows much more like a sermon than like a letter to particular hearers or a historical account such as the Gospels and Acts. It combines some of the most eloquent writing in the New Testament with deeply profound theological and Christological statements.

For both of us, it is our favorite book in the Bible, simply because it has done more to shape us into the persons we are today than any other. There are two qualities that make Hebrews stand out for us. First is its presentation of Jesus Christ. Hebrews dramatically reveals the humanity of Jesus, while at the same time powerfully arguing for his greatness and deity. No other biblical book paints so clear a picture of Jesus as a man of human weakness and at the same time as our mighty God. In the book of Hebrews, we see Jesus as the great high priest through whom we gain unlimited access to God. Hebrews presents the most exalted view of our Savior found in Scripture. And as Jesus said, "I, when I am lifted up from the earth, will draw all people to myself" (John 12:32), yet he is also the one who has been tempted in every way like us (Hebrews 4:15). This is what the book of Hebrews does.

The other reason we love this book with an unbridled passion is that, of all the books in the New Testament, it is the one that connects the New and Old Testaments most effectively. There is no close rival for second place in this respect. It is from Hebrews that we learn to interpret the items in the tabernacle, the laws, the sacrifices, the priesthood, the covenants, the festivals—indeed, nearly everything we find in the Hebrew Bible as types, prefigures and foreshadows of what we have in Christ. In Romans we learn that the Mosaic covenant was a foster parent for the Jews, admonishing them and reminding them how completely inadequate they were to have a relationship with God based on their own righteousness. In Hebrews we see how wonderful a foster parent and what a magnificent teacher the Old Testament was.

Another way to think of Hebrews is as the fifth gospel. The gospels are Matthew, Mark, Luke, John and Hebrews. Of course, Hebrews does not include a detailed account of Jesus' ministry, and it does not include an account of the death, burial and resurrection of our Lord, so it is not a classical gospel in that sense. But in another sense, a gospel is a revealed picture of Jesus. Each of the four classical Gospels gives us a unique picture of the Christ. Hebrews gives us a fifth. Matthew reveals Jesus as the one who fulfills the prophecies of the Old Testament and who satisfies and completes the law of Moses. Mark reveals Jesus as the one who powerfully announced the coming of the kingdom of God. Luke reveals him as the one who brings salvation even in this life, especially for the poor, the outcast, women and Gentiles. John reveals Jesus as the Son of God through his miracles and his I AM statements. Of course, Jesus is all of these things, and Hebrews gives us a yet another revelation of him. In Hebrews Jesus is the great high priest of God for all of his people. It is only in Hebrews that we see him as such. Of all the qualities of Jesus brought out in the book, it is his role as high priest of a new covenant that the Hebrew writer places at the forefront.

Although Hebrews gives us a picture of Jesus' unrivaled majesty and brings the Old and New Testaments together more than any other book does, neither of these was the reason it was written in the first place. The writer proclaims the purpose of the Book of Hebrews to us: it was given as a word of *paraklesis,* "exhortation" (Hebrews 13:22), a word that is also translated "encouragement." The book was written to exhort or encourage us. Hebrews certainly lives up to this statement, with its five warnings and five encouragements. The book is a resounding call for believers to strengthen their faith by focusing on Jesus, the great man, prophet, Messiah and God.

> *Strengthen your feeble arms and weak knees. "Make level paths for your feet."... Make every effort to live in peace with all men...be holy.... See to it that no one falls short of the grace of God and that no bitter root grows up.... See that no one is sexually immoral, or is godless like Esau. (Hebrews 12:12–16)*

If we heed the call of the writer of Hebrews to fix our eyes on Jesus, the beginner and completer of our faith, and if we accept wholeheartedly the exhortations found in this marvelous book, there is no doubt whatsoever that we will realize the goal envisioned in it, which is to enter the eternal Sabbath rest God has prepared for his people.

We are about to embark on a journey from which we will emerge as changed people. We cannot delve deeply into Hebrews without being transformed by this most amazing book. The power for our transformation is simple: it comes from the person Jesus Christ. How, then, does the writer present our Redeemer and Creator Jesus to us? And how does he turn this picture into a word of encouragement through which, if we accept it, we can be assured of our salvation? Before delving into this and before receiving the admonition to faithful living God has in store for us, let us consider the background, the theme, the audience and the style particular to the book of Hebrews.

Theme and Purpose

The writer of Hebrews has a single purpose in mind—one from which he (or she; but for simplicity we will not use both male and female pronouns) does not deviate in the slightest throughout the book. His purpose is to strengthen Christians who are weakening in their faith, so that they will make it to heaven. Although the technology was not invented at the time, we would say that the Hebrew writer was laser focused on this purpose. A perusal of the book will show immediately what the author is trying to accomplish, through statements like these: "So do not throw away your confidence; it will be richly rewarded" (Hebrews 10:35). "We want each of you to show this same diligence to the very end, so

> **The Purpose of Hebrews: To strengthen Christians who are weakening in their faith so that they will make it to heaven.**

that what you hope for may be fully realized. We do not want you to become lazy, but to imitate those who through faith and patience inherit what has been promised" (Hebrews 6:11–12). "Therefore, since the promise of entering his rest still stands, let us be careful that none of you be found to have fallen short of it" (Hebrews 4:1). "See to it that no one falls short of the grace of God and that no bitter root grows up to cause trouble and defile many" (Hebrews 12:15).

We should not be at all surprised to learn that the theme of Hebrews fits hand in glove with its purpose. There are things that we need to do to be assured of our salvation—to make it to the promised land. Hebrews exhorts us in several ways to do them. Hopefully, as you read the book you will accept the admonitions and you will do these things that will keep you on the path to heaven. However, doing them is not the ultimate key to making it to God's promised land. What single idea does the writer of Hebrews believe will help his hearers get to heaven? Quite simple: we need to fix our eyes on Jesus, the pioneer and perfecter of our faith. The theme of Hebrews is the greatness of Christ as our high priest and the author of our salvation. The core of the argument expounded in Hebrews is a

> ## The theme of Hebrews: The greatness of Christ as our high priest and the author of our salvation.

presentation of the preeminence of Jesus. The outline of Hebrews is basically this: the writer gives us a series of reasons that Jesus is superior to particuar things the Jews had in the old covenant; therefore, he admonishes us to persevere in our faith in particular ways so that we will certainly be saved. The writer of Hebrews comes back again and again to Jesus and his superiority, using this to motivate us to accept his admonitions.

Various books in the Bible contain a key word or phrase crucial to understanding what is being said. In the case of Hebrews, this key Greek word is *kreitton*, which can be translated as "superior to," "better than" or "greater than." The word appears twelve times in the book and is essential to the argument throughout. Jesus is greater than... The author of Hebrews argues the superiority of Jesus over the things found in Judaism in every conceivable manner. Consider some of the ways in which the Hebrew writer presents Jesus as superior to what is found in the old covenant:

1. Jesus is greater than the prophets (1:1–3).

2. Jesus is greater than the angels (1:4–1:14, 2:5–9).

3. Jesus is greater than Moses (3:1–6).

4. Jesus is greater than Joshua (4:8).

5. Jesus is greater than the high priest (4:14–5:10).

6. Jesus is greater than Abraham (6:13–18, 7:4–5).

7. Jesus' priesthood is greater than the priesthood of Aaron (6:20–

7:28).

8. Jesus' covenant is greater than the covenant of Moses (8:1–13).

9. Jesus dwells in a greater, heavenly tabernacle (9:1–11).

10. Jesus offers a greater sacrifice (9:12–10:18).

Through Jesus we have superior blessings (7:7), a superior hope (7:19), superior possessions (10:34), a superior country (11:16), a superior resurrection (11:35), superior promises (11:39–40) and access to superior blood (12:24). The bottom line is this: Christianity is superior to any other religion. It is worthy of our enduring suffering and lifelong devotion. This is the theme of Hebrews, and it is what will make it possible for us to accept the exhortations we find there and put them into our lives, and thus to achieve the goal of our faith, the salvation of our souls.

Audience

As we study the book of Hebrews, it will be essential to be aware of the audience that the writer has in mind. This determines again and again what he says and how he says it. If we forget the audience, we will not understand how the writer chooses his examples, and we will often miss the point he is trying to make. So, who is the all-important audience of Hebrews? Of course, Hebrews is written for Christians generally, but the audience that the writer seems to have in mind is Jewish Christians who were tempted to give up on Christianity. Some are in danger of turning back and losing their salvation. The context and the examples the author uses hint to us that these older Jewish disciples are considering blending back into the Jewish community from which they were called out.

The numerous Old Testament references in the book clearly speak to an audience familiar with the Hebrew Scriptures and the history of the Jewish people. Hebrews quotes the Old Testament more times (sixty-one, to be exact) than any other writing in the New Testament outside of Matthew. The scriptures quoted are primarily from the Septuagint, the Greek Old Testament, possibly pointing to a Greek-speaking Hellenistic Jewish community outside of Palestine.

These Christians have been around awhile (Hebrews 5:12). They have done great things in their faith are now tempted to look back. They are spiritually and emotionally tired. Despite all they have accomplished and the great victories they have witnessed, the question is coming into their minds: *Is it worth it?* Maybe the audience of Hebrews is you. Perhaps you can relate to these mature but worn-out followers of Jesus. Instead of doing more and more for Christ, you are doing less and less. You are hanging in there spiritually, but the honest truth is that you have not been growing. You are tempted to look back, and your faith is not where it was in the past. If this is the case, then decide right now that you will allow Hebrews to let you look intently at Jesus, and resolve to put the exhortations in the book into practice.

We can get a sense of the audience from Hebrews 10:32–34. The writer addresses his audience directly with the following admonition:

> Remember those earlier days after you had received the light, when you endured in a great conflict full of suffering. Sometimes you were publicly exposed to insult and persecution; at other times you stood side by side with those who were so treated. You suffered along with those in prison and joyfully accepted the confiscation of your property, because you knew that you yourselves had better and lasting possessions.

These were not weak disciples. They had stood strong and endured persecution for the name of Christ. But notice this: the writer says, "because you knew." That word "knew" is in the past tense. In the light of the cares of this world, these Jewish Christians have lost sight of the "better and lasting possessions" they have in Christ. They are focusing on the outward things of religion and losing sight of the reason they left Judaism in the first place. What was that reason? Why did they leave the comfort of the law of Moses? The Hebrew writer reminds them over and over again: it was Jesus Christ.

We are given further evidence of the audience of Hebrews. On the one hand, the author addresses Jewish history with great respect and reverence. On the other hand, he makes the clearest possible statement condemning those who turn back to the old covenant, because it is "obsolete" (Hebrews 8:13) and involves "useless rituals" (Hebrews 9:14 GNT).

The Jewish understanding that God is holy and cannot be approached by man is prominent in Hebrews. The book is written from a point of view of deep respect for God. The hearers are reminded that he said, "No one may see me and live" (Exodus 33:20). Only the high priest and only on the Day of Atonement and only for a few brief moments could anyone be in the presence of the Holy One. The likelihood that the audience of the book is Jewish is also important for understanding the significance the author places on the role of high priest, something that non-Jewish Christians would not be all that much concerned about.

Another hint as to the audience is found in the references to worship. It explains the mystery of why the author mentions the tabernacle eight times but does not refer to the temple even once. A Gentile convert would be well aware of the temple in Jerusalem but may never even have heard of the tabernacle that was moved about in the wilderness. The tabernacle had not existed for over a thousand years when Hebrews was written. Again and again we will see that the writer of Hebrews explains things Christians already know but does so through the lens of the Old Testament. It is clear that the author held a masterful grasp of the Hebrew Bible and Jewish theology.

Why this focus on a Jewish Christian audience? Why were they, in particular, tempted to turn back to the religion they had left behind? Christianity was initially seen as a sect of Judaism, which was a politically accepted religion in the Roman Empire. In the first generation of the Church, the followers had a tenuous safety net within Judaism. By the second half of the first century, however, Roman rulers were beginning to realize that Christians were not the same as Jews. In fact, by the 60s the majority of Christians were converted Gentiles. They had never been Jews. As time went by, Christians were singled out from the Jews and persecuted as part of a new and unacceptable religion. This transition was happening at the time Hebrews was written. Within less than a generation of the writing of this book, Christianity was outlawed throughout the Roman Empire under Domitian. This led to a quandary for the Christians who did come from a Jewish background. Were they going to self-identify as Jewish or as Christian? To be Jewish meant relative prosperity and safety. To be identified as Christian meant being ostracized, labeled as a fanatic, and possibly even arrested and killed. Hebrews issues a clear and strong warning against those who were tempted to hide behind their Judaism to the point that they might ultimately deny Jesus: "How shall we escape if we ignore so great a salvation?" (Hebrews 2:3).

The warnings in Hebrews against ignoring this great salvation apply to us today as well, although the specifics are different. We are not tempted to hide behind "the temple of the Lord, the temple of the Lord" (Jeremiah 7:4), but we are sorely tempted to blend in to a culturally acceptable brand of

Christianity. We do not want to feel like foreigners and strangers (Hebrews 11:13). We are looking back to the "country" of lax Christianity that we left (Hebrews 11:15–16). If you have been slipping into a comfortable form of Christianity, prepare to feel uncomfortable as you read this book.

Another suggestion about the audience of the book is found in Hebrews 13:24: "Those from Italy send you their greetings." Unfortunately, this is not quite as helpful as we might like, because it could be mean that the writer is with Jewish Christians in Italy, writing to a group elsewhere, or it could be that the author is with a group of Jewish Christians expelled from Rome under Claudius in AD 49, who are now living outside of Italy. So, either the audience is Jewish Christians who have now returned to Italy under Nero, after the expulsion, or hellenized Jewish Christians who were among those expelled, but who are now living outside of Italy.

One more note about the audience: commentators from a Calvinist perspective have a hard time discussing the recipients of the book. The reason is that the Calvinist is convinced of a strong predestination—one under which we humans have no part in choosing whether we will be saved or not. We are saved by "faith alone," and that faith is imparted to us by God. Therefore, to the majority of evangelical believers, once a person is saved, they cannot lose their salvation. This is called the doctrine of perseverance, popularly known as "once saved, always saved." The problem is that we will see dozens of passages in Hebrews warning against losing our salvation. If the principle audience of Hebrews is Jewish Christians who cannot lose their salvation, then to whom are these passages addressed?

Here is what committed Calvinist commentators do: they propose a secondary audience. This supposed smaller but significant group of recipients of Hebrews are Jews who have been hanging around the Church for many years but have never been baptized. When, therefore, the Hebrew writer says something such as "It is impossible for those who have once been enlightened, who have tasted the heavenly gift, who have shared in the Holy Spirit, who have tasted the goodness of the word of God and the powers of the coming age, and who have fallen away, to be brought back to repentance," mainstream evangelical commentators propose that the audience for these comments consists of men and women who have been attending church for many years but have not yet been saved. They claim that "having been enlightened" means having heard the gospel, not having been saved.

This theory has many problems. First, there is no internal evidence in

Hebrews for a secondary audience of the unsaved. Second, the words in the above passage are rather obviously describing saved people. This secondary-audience theory is an ad hoc hypothesis (one created, not because of the evidence, but to explain away the evidence). Its quality speaks for itself. We will discuss the doctrine of predestination and perseverance of the saints in our treatment of the text.

Author

We know a good deal about the audience of Hebrews; it would be helpful to know about the author as well. Unfortunately for us, he did not sign his letter, or if he did, it has not come down to us, so it is not known who wrote Hebrews. Its authorship is a mystery that has been the subject of much speculation almost from the time the book was written. Here are the facts as we have them: By the Middle Ages both the Eastern and the Western Churches regarded Hebrews as one of Paul's works. As early as the late fourth century, Augustine claimed that the book was written by Paul. As early as the third century, it was considered part of the Pauline writings by many. However, there is reason to think that Augustine made this claim, not because of evidence, but in order to impart greater apostolic authority to the book. Pauline authorship was the accepted tradition of the early Reformers as well. The original edition of the King James Bible called it "The Epistle of Paul the Apostle to the Hebrews." However, over time, most scholars have come to dismiss Pauline authorship as very unlikely. Why is that?

There are two main lines of reasoning that lead to the conclusion that it is quite unlikely that Paul wrote Hebrews. First is the fact that the very earliest witnesses did not believe Paul wrote it, and second, the style of the book points more strongly to him not being the author. As far as the early witnesses go, we have Tertullian, who near the end of the second century suggested that it was common knowledge that Hebrews was not written by Paul. He proposed that perhaps Barnabas wrote the book, noting that Barnabas, not Paul, would be more likely to write in such elegant Greek. The most famous opinion of all on the authorship is that of Origen. In the first half of the third century he said, perhaps with a bit of exasperation, "God only knows" who wrote Hebrews. Although we will do a bit of speculating here on the author, probably the wisest choice is to agree with Origen.

As already noted, there is evidence from the style of writing of Hebrews. The language and vocabulary of the book are strikingly different from Paul's letters. The Greek is more elegant, more cultured and reveals a deeper vocabulary than Paul shows in his letters. Of the 4,942 words in the book, the writer uses 1,038 different words, 169 of which are only found in Hebrews. That alone is not absolute proof, as a practiced author can purposefully alter his writing style for thematic reasons. Besides, one can propose that Paul wrote the book but that it was substantially edited by an associate with a more sophisticated style of Greek. But there is more to this question of writing style. Perhaps most significant to the question is the fact that the author does not claim to have known Jesus personally. The author appears to have received eyewitness accounts of Jesus from others. He was converted by someone who had firsthand knowledge of Jesus: "This salvation, which was first announced by the Lord, was confirmed to us by those who heard him" (Hebrews 2:3). Another argument against Paul as an author is that he never mentions Jesus as a priest in any of his known writings, yet this is the principle theme of Hebrews.

Putting aside Paul for a moment, what can we know about the author of Hebrews? We can easily surmise by the Old Testament references that the writer was Jewish and well acquainted with Judaism. He quotes from the Greek Septuagint, not the Hebrew. Likewise, we can gather from the eloquent Greek that this person was highly educated in a Hellenistic culture. There are also a number of nautical references that would indicate someone from a port city or having experience with shipping. Likely candidates that have been proposed include Apollos, a native of Alexandria (a port city) and a Greek-speaking Jew who was well known for being an eloquent speaker. It is not a stretch to propose that Apollos the great orator would also be a great writer. Some, with Tertullian, have suggested Barnabas, a native of the island of Cyprus who was Jewish and probably educated in Greek. As noted, the letter of Hebrews calls itself a word of *paraklesis,* which is translated "encouragement" (Hebrews 12:5) or "exhortation" (Hebrews 13:22). Perhaps it is coincidence (or perhaps not) that Barnabas was known to be called the "son of *paraklesis.*" Was this a hint from the author?

The most intriguing candidate suggested, and Robert's personal favorite, is Priscilla. She was a hellenized Greek-speaking Jew as well. To propose a female author would perhaps answer the question as to why the identity of the writer has been clouded in mystery from almost the beginning. The important leadership role Priscilla had in the early Church is illustrated by the fact that when she and her husband are mentioned, Priscilla is generally named first. This cannot be an accident, and it implies that she was the power person—the stronger voice and the more influential leader of the two. All of us know great spiritual Christian couples for whom this is the case. Priscilla was certainly a strong disciple who was a first-century equivalent of a woman "in the ministry" of the Church. Evidence against Priscilla as author is that the author refers to himself with a male pronoun in Hebrews 11:32.

A minor point to note is that the author may have been in Italy when the letter was written: "Those from Italy send you their greetings" (Hebrews 13:24b). On the other hand, it is also possible that a group from Italy was present at the writing of the letter and they sent their greetings through the author to a community of disciples in Italy. It is worth noting that many Italian Jews such as Priscilla and Aquila were forced to leave Rome in AD 49 (Acts18:2) by the persecution of Claudius.

Of the potential authors, the one we know enough about who also best fits the traits we can glean from the book is probably Apollos. If he is not the writer, then his biography is similar to the writer's. It would not be an overstatement to say that the author was someone *like* Apollos. Our conclusion on the author of this wonderful book is to return to the statement of Origen: "Only God knows."

For modern readers, speculation about the author is interesting and perhaps somewhat helpful, but the key question is the inspiration and authority of this document. The existence of questions about who wrote Hebrews does not in the least diminish the role of the Holy Spirit in inspiring the writing. It is the personalities of the authors that give a unique flavor to each of the different writings in the Bible. However, the uniqueness of each author does not negate that the canonical books in the Bible are inspired by God. Here is the bottom line for us: Hebrews is inspired by God. We know this because we have faith in God that he used the apostles and the very early church leaders to choose those books that God wanted to be included in the New Testament canon.

One reason to believe that Hebrews is inspired and authoritative results from our faith that God could oversee the formation of his Bible. Let us go beyond this. We propose that if one were to remove the question of authorship from the twenty-nine books of the New Testament and simply lay them side by side, comparing their qualities, then Hebrews would stand out on its merits alone as the most obviously inspired of all the books in the New Testament, because of its beauty, elegance, insight, depth, consistency with the rest of the Bible and for many other reasons. How could anyone question the inspiration of this amazing book?

For prophecy never had its origin in the human will, but prophets, though human, spoke from God as they were carried along by the Holy Spirit. (2 Peter 1:21)

Date

The date of writing of Hebrews has some significance to our understanding of the book because of what it says about Judaism and specifically about the temple. Most likely the book was composed somewhere between AD 60 and 70. It was likely composed after AD 60, because the audience is second-generation Christians who have been in the faith for at least twenty years and probably more. The writing was almost certainly completed before AD 70, because it is apparent from the book that the temple in Jerusalem was still standing when it was written. In AD 69 Roman troops under Vespasian surrounded the city, and in AD 70, under Vespasian's son Titus, the walls were breached, the city was burned and the temple was taken right down to the ground. Pagan sacrifice was offered on the site of the temple. All of this had been prophesied by Daniel (Daniel 9:26–27) and Jesus (Matthew 24:15–21). We can assume that the writer of Hebrews was aware of these prophecies of the destruction of Jerusalem and the final demise of the Jewish sacrificial system.

We know that the temple still stood when Hebrews was written, because it is described in the present tense in the book. In Hebrews 8:13 the author tells us with authority concerning the old covenant that it is "obsolete; and what is obsolete and outdated will soon disappear." It is an intriguing possibility that when Hebrews was written, the city may have already been surrounded by the Roman armies and the writer was talking about current events.

If we are right, then the date of the book is quite significant to the message. God is telling his people that turning back to relying on Jewish ritual in order to avoid suffering would be an especially bad idea if the very system of sacrifice they were so proud of was on the verge of collapsing, never to recover.

Vocabulary and Style

As has already been said, the language is unanimously considered by scholars to be the most elegant Greek in the New Testament. Although written in beautiful, often almost lyrical, language, the book was clearly written in the form of a sermon and intended by its author to be read aloud in front of a group. We suggest that as you study Hebrews you occasionally stop and read sections out loud. You may want to let the other members of your household know what you are doing so they will not think you are talking to yourself! Reading aloud helps bring the impact of Hebrews alive.

The oral character of the writing is indicated by the choice of verbs in the book. For example, "It is not to angels that he has subjected the world to come, about which we are speaking" (Hebrews 2:5). "We have much to say about this, but it is hard to make it clear to you because you no longer try to understand" (Hebrews 5:11). "Even though we speak like this, dear friends, we are convinced of better things in your case" (Hebrews 6:9). "Now the main point of what we are saying is this..." (Hebrews 8:1). "And what more shall I say? I do not have time to tell about Gideon..." (Hebrews 11:32). In all of these the writer uses a conversational tone and even conversational words.

Hebrews does not begin with the usual greetings and salutations and only has a few comments to individuals at the very end. It is therefore not a letter. When the book is analyzed, it is easily outlined in the form of a sermon. No other book in the Bible is written quite this way. We can see the writer's first and second point about the superiority of Jesus, followed by an exhortation, then his third reason why Jesus is superior to an aspect of Judaism, followed by his second exhortation, then his fourth and fifth examples of Jesus' superiority, followed by his third exhortation, and so on. As any good preacher does, the writer then summarizes his points in the second part of chapter 12 (vv. 18–29) and finishes out the sermon in chapter 13 with a few closing exhortations and reminders to his hearers.

Things to Look For in Hebrews

There are a few repeating patterns in the book of Hebrews which it will be helpful to have in mind as we begin our study of the text. First and most obvious is that you should look for things that are great about Jesus. When teaching this book we tend to run out of superlatives and end up resorting to a thesaurus. Jesus is unique. He is astounding, glorious, fantastic, wonderful, superior and, of course, the overused awesome. But really, he is awesome in the original sense of the word, and the covenant he is the author of is equally superior, grander, loftier and a lot of other really great words.

Second, you should look for the exhortations and warnings. At the risk of giving away the movie before it starts, here are some of the major exhortations in Hebrews:

1. Pay careful attention (2:1–4).
2. Make every effort (3:7–4:11).
3. Move on to maturity (5:11–6:12).
4. Draw near to God (10:19–31).
5. Do not shrink back (10:32–39).
6. Live by faith (11:1–40).
7. Persevere by looking at Jesus (12:1–29).

A third thing to be on the lookout for in Hebrews is the writer's use of types, prefigures and foreshadows from the Old Testament of things found in the New Testament. Like Paul (in Galatians 4:21–31, for example), the writer of Hebrews uses objects, people and historical events in the Old Testament as physical examples of a spiritual reality found in the new covenant. He considers not just predictive prophecies but the entire Old Testament as foretelling the New. To the Hebrew writer, the Old Testament is a shadow, and the reality is found in Jesus. He tells us that the very law of Moses itself was merely a foreshadow of the things we have in Christ (Hebrews 10:1).[1] We have already mentioned the great number of Old Testament citations in Hebrews. If we add the use of prefigures and foreshadows to this list, the number of Old Testament references becomes much longer still. In Hebrews we gain overwhelming evidence that the Old Testament is inspired by God, and at the same time, the Old Testament comes alive through Hebrews more than in any other New Testament book. Here we see illustrated in broad strokes and in great detail the claim of Jesus about the entire Hebrew Bible that "these are the very Scriptures that testify about me" (John 5:39).

Another feature of Hebrews is the use of imagery of Christians as wanderers, pilgrims and wayfarers. We are people for whom this world is not our home. We should not expect to fit in, and we should not look back to the country from which we came. Our life is one of separation and hardship. The failed nerve of some of the audience of Hebrews is explained by their lack of focus on our heavenly home. We should have confidence in the future, not because of anything the world has to offer, but because of our expectation of a better home—a Sabbath rest with God. This confidence should form the basis for our faithful actions in the present.

One more thing we want to encourage you to be looking for in

Hebrews is the use of words that are uncommon in the New Testament but that would be familiar to a Jew in New Testament times. A few words used often in Hebrews and often in the Old Testament, but rarely in the New Testament outside Hebrews, include "tabernacle," "high priest," "covenant," "offerings," "sacrifice" and "blood." There is clearly a pattern here. All of these are items in Jewish priestly worship. Be prepared to receive a bit of a primer on the Jewish religious cult as you study Hebrews, being aware that all of these things are replaced by something much greater that is found in Jesus.

There are three other words found much in Hebrews but not frequently elsewhere in the New Testament. They are "perfect" (Greek: teleios), found fifteen times; "superior" (Greek: kreitton) and "greater than/more than" (Greek: polys). The Hebrew writer exhausted his vocabulary in describing Jesus and the covenant we have in him. He is perfect, superior to and greater than everyone and everything that came before him and that will come after him.

Outline

We will provide two outlines of Hebrews. The first is probably pretty close to the one that the writer of the sermon may have composed. It has the added advantage of wonderfully illustrating the theme and purpose of the book. The second is probably not the one the Hebrew writer would have used, but it may be helpful for us as we make our way through this incredible book.

Outline #1:

1. Jesus is greater than the prophets (1:1–3)
2. Jesus is greater than the angels (1:4–1:14, 2:5–9)
3. Exhortation #1: Pay careful attention (2:1–4)
4. Jesus, a perfect priest through suffering (2:10–18)
5. Jesus is greater than Moses (3:1–6)
6. Exhortation #2: Make every effort (3:7–4:13)
7. Jesus is greater than the high priest (4:14–5:10)
8. Exhortation #3: Move on to maturity (5:11–6:12)
9. Jesus is greater than Abraham (6:13–20a)

10. Jesus' priesthood is like that of Melchizedek and is greater than the priesthood of Aaron (6:20b–7:28)
11. Jesus' covenant is greater than the covenant of Moses (8:1–13)
12. Jesus dwells in a greater, heavenly tabernacle (9:1–11)
13. Jesus offers a greater sacrifice (9:12–10:18)
14. Exhortation #4: Draw near to God, do not shrink back: The peril of rebellion against God (10:19–39)
15. Exhortation #5: Live by faith (11:1–40)
16. Look to Jesus (12:1–17)
17. Summary (12:18–29)
18. Final exhortations (13:1–25)

Outline #2

Hebrews 1–6 – The person Jesus Christ
Hebrews 7–10:18 – The ministry of Jesus Christ
Hebrews 10:19–13:25 – Exhortations

Let us now move into the text of the book of Hebrews.

End Notes _____

1. John Oakes has published a book on types, prefigures and foreshadows in the Old Testament and their fulfillment in the New. It is John Oakes, *From Shadow to Reality* (Spring, Texas: Illumination Publishers, 2004). It is available at www.ipibooks.com.

_____ Chapter 1 _____

Jesus Is Greater than the Prophets
Hebrews 1:1–3

T he one delivering this remarkable sermon starts us off with a bang. He gets into his theme in the very first verse: Jesus is something to behold. He is greater than the prophets.

> _In the past God spoke to our ancestors through the prophets at many times and in various ways, but in these last days he has spoken to us by his Son, whom he appointed heir of all things, and through whom also he made the universe. The Son is the radiance of God's glory and the exact representation of his being, sustaining all things by his powerful word. After he had provided purification for sins, he sat down at the right hand of the Majesty in heaven._ (Hebrews 1:1–3)

The first paragraph of Hebrews is a masterpiece of Greek. The language is poetic and complex. The first sentence contains five words starting with the letter "p." Just try to make a theological statement using five words that begin with the letter "p" and see what you come up with! The phrase "many times and in various ways" (_polymeros kai polytropos_) is classical language setting the tone of Hebrews as poetic literature.

God has certainly spoken to us at many times and in many ways. He has spoken to us through history, poetry, prophecy and proverb. He has spoken to us through kings (David, Solomon), patriarchs (Moses, Job), poets (Asaph), farmers (Amos), scribes (the authors of the historical books), priests (Ezra), prophets, prophetesses (Deborah) and, yes, even government administrators (Nehemiah).

William Barclay in his commentary on Hebrews describes the role of each of the prophets as producing a fragment of God's message. The prophets were highly esteemed and respected, yet each one carried only a single sentence of God's over all missive to man. Some spoke of repentance, like Jonah; others spoke of God's holiness, like Isaiah; of his grace, like Hosea;

of his justice, like Amos; or of his wisdom, like Solomon. Each conveyed an aspect of God's character in his prophecy. Jesus, in contrast, was more than a fragment of God's message—he is the entire book! Like each key on a piano, each prophet had his tone, but Jesus is the keyboard. Like a musician, each prophet played his part, but Jesus is the entire orchestra. The prophets brought the message, but Jesus *is* the message.

In saying this, the author of Hebrews is stressing that the New Testament is in continuity with the Old, rather than emphasizing the difference between them. The message brought by Jesus is the consummation of what was begun in the Old Testament. He is the one who fulfilled the Law and the Prophets (Matthew 5:17). In Christ we move from promise and anticipation to fulfillment. As the writer of Hebrews expresses it in one place, "God had planned something better for us so that only together with us would they be made perfect" (Hebrews 11:40).

The phrase "in these last days" is language familiar to the first-century Christians. It is found frequently in the Septuagint Greek translation of the Old Testament. Since the Day of Pentecost, we have been living in the last days (Acts 2:16–17; 1 Peter 1:20; 1 Corinthians 10:11). The point is made that in these final days God no longer uses prophets; he sends his Son and heir Jesus to speak for him. Jesus is compared to the prophets but is vastly greater than they are. We are in the final dispensation of God's plan. The way the Hebrew writer puts it, "But he has appeared once for all at the culmination of the ages" (Hebrews 9:26).

Hebrews 1:2–3 is some of the loveliest Greek prose in the entire New Testament. In this section, the writer summarizes in stunning beauty how truly great our Savior Jesus Christ is. This passage is parallel to the description of Jesus by Paul in Colossians 1:15–19. First, Jesus is the heir of all things. Who is the heir? The Son. He gets it all, and if we are adopted as his brothers and sisters, then we are coheirs with Christ (Romans 8:17). This privilege is of incalculable value: we share in the inheritance.

Add to this the fact that Jesus is the one through whom the entire universe has been made. The way John put it, "Without him nothing was made that has been made" (John 1:3). This is power beyond our ability to conceive of. Our high priest Jesus is Creator; he is God.

Not only that, Jesus is the "radiance" or *apaugasma* of God's glory. *Apaugasma* can either mean the light that shines forth or the light that is reflected. Jesus is the one who shines forth. He is the principal means through which God's glory is revealed to humankind. To the extent that

God can be seen by human beings without them being destroyed by the radiance, that is what we have in Jesus: "We have seen his glory, the glory of the one and only Son" (John 1:14). He is the light of the world. Let us take time to gaze at Jesus, the shining radiance of God's glory.

The next concept is a beautiful one. Jesus is the "exact representation" or *charakter* of God. The Greek word here comes from the seal or impression imprinted in wax used to identify the sender of a gift or letter. Documents were sealed with wax, and a person's image or insignia was pressed on the hot wax, leaving an impression that clearly identified the sender. Jesus is the exact image of God. Again, to the extent that God can be seen, to the degree that his nature can be visible, we see him in Christ—in his spirit, his treatment of individuals, his attitude toward suffering, his love for the lost, his patience, his wisdom and much more. John writes, "No one has ever seen God, but the one and only Son, who is himself God and is in closest relationship with the Father, has made him known" (John 1:18). In all of our searching for God, we never found him. Instead, he came here and revealed himself to us. This is Jesus. This is what makes Christianity distinct from absolutely any religion of human invention. No one would have thought this up, yet it is what God has done in Christ.

Furthermore, the author of Hebrews reveals that "all things" are sustained by the power of Jesus' words. He does not merely state that Jesus is powerful. God tells us that *all* power comes from Jesus! He created the laws of nature and he keeps them working. The power to keep the sun shining for five billion years, to provide energy to a nuclear plant and to keep a heart beating for eighty years all come from Jesus and his word. We could not live or exist for even a fraction of a second without Jesus. All life on our planet depends on him. Jesus is the beginning (Creator), middle (sustainer) and end (inheritor) of all things.

But we are not done. Not only does the power to sustain life come from Jesus, he also provided the purification for sins we so desperately needed so that we might truly live life. Of all the attributes of Jesus described in Hebrews, this is the one that the book is about. This was the last act of Jesus on the earth. It was the principle reason, although not the only reason, he came in the flesh.

Only then—only after affording us purification for sin—did he sit at the right hand of God, reigning with him in his glory in the heavenly tabernacle. This is a reference to Psalm 110:1: "*Adonai* said to my Lord, 'Sit at my right hand until I make your enemies a footstool for your feet.'" Our evangelist will return to the subject of Jesus' service on our behalf at the right hand of God in chapter 9. He closes his overwhelming description of Jesus by concluding that he is, therefore, much superior to the angels. But that is our next section.

End Notes _____

2. Septuagint and Dead Sea Scrolls.

_ Chapter 2 ____

Jesus Is Greater Than the Angels
Hebrews 1:4–14

Jesus is greater than the prophets—infinitely so. He did not just bring the message, he is the message. Now our author moves on to the second element of Judaism over which Jesus is far superior. Jesus is greater than the angels; he is "as much superior to the angels as the name he has inherited is superior to theirs" (Hebrews 1:4). There were strongly held beliefs among the Jews about the role of angels at this time. These highly regarded beings, are known as *aggeloi* in Greek and מַלְאָךְ [malach] in Hebrew. Angels are messengers of God, which is what the word *aggeloi* means. They were esteemed by the Jews as the only beings holy enough to speak directly to God and be in his presence. It was believed that it was angels who brought the law to Moses on Sinai. In this next section of Hebrews it is made clear that Jesus is far above the angels, in a class by himself. The author uses a series of Old Testament quotes highlighting the differences between Jesus' relationship with God and that of the angels, explaining the superiority of Jesus to the angels.

> *For to which of the angels did God ever say,*
>
> *"You are my Son;*
> > *today I have become your Father"?* [quoting Psalm 2:7]
>
> *Or again,*
> > *"I will be his Father,*
> > *and he will be my Son"?* [2 Samuel 7:14]
>
> *And again, when God brings his firstborn into the world, he says,*
> > *"Let all God's angels worship him."* [Deuteronomy 32:43 LXX and DSS²]
>
> *In speaking of the angels he says,*
> > *"He makes his angels spirits,*
> > *and his servants flames of fire."* [Psalm 104:4]

But about the Son he says,

> *"Your throne, O God, will last for ever and ever;*
>> *a scepter of justice will be the scepter of your kingdom.*
> *You have loved righteousness and hated wickedness;*
>> *therefore God, your God, has set you above your companions*
>> *by anointing you with the oil of joy."* [Psalm 45:6–7]

He also says,

> *"In the beginning, Lord, you laid the foundations of the earth,*
>> *and the heavens are the work of your hands.*
> *They will perish, but you remain;*
>> *they will all wear out like a garment.*
> *You will roll them up like a robe;*
>> *like a garment they will be changed.*
> *But you remain the same,*
>> *and your years will never end."* [Psalm 102:25–27]

To which of the angels did God ever say,

> *"Sit at my right hand*
>> *until I make your enemies*
>> *a footstool for your feet"?* [Psalm 110:1]

Are not all angels ministering spirits sent to serve those who will inherit salvation? (Hebrews 1:5–14)

The scriptures woven together here highlight promises concerning Jesus throughout the ages. They demonstrate that his coming to save humankind was not just an afterthought when things got out of hand. It was God's intention from the beginning to send his Son, and his angels were merely messengers preparing the way for the Son to come. He was central to the plan all along. He is the fulfillment of the Law and his ministry marks the final victory of God. A person cannot be right with God and be wrong with Jesus. None of these things are true of angels.

The writer of Hebrews uses the scriptures above to point out several ways in which the angels are inferior to Jesus.

1. A Greater Name

First of all, Jesus has a much better name than the angels. They are called messenger. He is called Son. Ancient Near East peoples put much significance into a name. Beyond a mere label, the name was identified with the thing named and was thought of as having power in and of itself. In a royal hierarchy, who has more honor and power, a messenger or the son of the king? Jesus has a much greater name.

2. A Greater Role

Angels are messengers, and the message is Jesus. Being a messenger for God is quite an honor, but which should we pay attention to, the messenger or the message?

3. Angels Change, Jesus Does Not

The scripture shows that angels change. To the Greeks, anything that changes is lesser than anything unchanging. The angels are winds and fires (v. 7). These are things that come and go and that change rapidly. In the Jewish apocryphal work 4 Esdras 8:21 angels are described in a way reminiscent of Hebrews 1:7: "God, before whom the heavenly host stand in terror and at your word change to wind and fire." In a rabbinic homily an angel says, "God changes us every hour. Sometimes he makes us fire, other times wind." By comparison, Jesus is eternal and unchanging. His throne will last forever and ever. As the psalmist said, and as the Hebrew writer applies to Jesus, "you remain the same, and your years will never end." Why would we give our attention to angels?

4. Angels Will Perish

To the Greek mind, the great things were both unchanging and eternal. Angels will perish (v. 11). They wear out. They become tired. In the psalm the earth is being discussed, but the writer of Hebrews is applying this to angels. Jesus is eternal, and how much greater is something eternal than anything temporary? What is infinity divided by any number? Infinity.

5. Angels Are Ministering Spirits

Again, it is a great honor to be a ministering spirit for God—to communicate his message to his people. Angels are ministering spirits (v. 14), but Jesus is the one ministered to. Why would the Jews want to worship the worshipper? They should worship Jesus, the one who sits at

God's right hand. Jesus is vastly superior to the angels. (This theme will be revisited in Hebrews 2:5–9, which we will cover in the next chapter.)

Chapter 3

Exhortation #1: Pay Careful Attention
Hebrews 2:1–9

We must pay the most careful attention, therefore, to what we have heard, so that we do not drift away. For since the message spoken through angels was binding, and every violation and disobedience received its just punishment, how shall we escape if we ignore so great a salvation? This salvation, which was first announced by the Lord, was confirmed to us by those who heard him. God also testified to it by signs, wonders and various miracles, and by gifts of the Holy Spirit distributed according to his will. (Hebrews 2:1–4)

Chapter 2 begins with the first of five stern exhortations found in Hebrews. Each is a warning concerning something that could cause us to lose our faith in Jesus and eventually our salvation. The five warnings are in Hebrews 2:1–4, 3:7–19, 5:11–6:12, 10:19–39 and 12:14–29. They flow like a five-point sermon. The first exhortation is to pay attention! How do you feel when someone tells you to pay attention? *"Who, me?"* That is the problem. When we are not paying attention, we are not attentive to the fact that we are not paying attention. Do not lose focus or "space out" on something so incredibly important. Pay attention to what? To Jesus, of course, but in this case we are being admonished to pay attention "to what we have heard," to "the message" delivered to us, and to "so great a salvation" that has been offered to us.

In this first sentence two nautical terms are used to illustrate what is being talked about. In the phrase "pay the most careful attention," the word used is *prosechein*. This word means to be on guard and be on the lookout. It was a term used by a sailor to refer to standing watch. It was the nautical term for anchoring or mooring a ship. This term would stand out to the hearer as a forceful command. As Christians we must stand guard and remain anchored to Jesus. The next word to note is *pararrein*. This is another nautical term, which means to slip or drift away. A ship that has been improperly moored or anchored will drift as it is carried away by the tide. When we drift from the mooring, we are likely to be destroyed on the rocks. It is not a sudden disappearance, but a slow slipping away. If a boat goes adrift in a river, the passengers can be floating downstream without even knowing it, until they look at the land and realize that they have been moving with the current. It is that way in our Christian life. In this case, the "land" we should be looking at is the message of our salvation.

Christians do not usually fall away suddenly. Falling away usually begins with a carelessness about our spiritual wellbeing. A weak Christian drifts by allowing themself to make compromises in their spiritual discipline. It starts with small things like allowing daily Bible reading to slide. Prayer times get skipped or become mechanical recital, void of heart. Modern life is incredibly busy, perhaps busier than ever in the history of the human race, which is ironic considering the technological advances we have made that should make life easier. Yet it seems the more we advance the busier we get. If we do not aggressively fight for time with God, life squeezes him out of our schedules. As a person is slipping away, temptations become stronger. Once we begin to give in to temptation, we also begin isolating ourselves from God and his people. As with any relationship, time together is a necessity. Communication is a relational requirement.

Distance is always the devil's playground. As God becomes farther away, we can even begin to judge him instead of acknowledging that he is our righteous judge—we decide that he is unfair, that he asks too much of us, etc. Sin no longer seems so wrong, and Satan is always ready to provide a justification for it. Where once we readily shared our struggles with close friends, lack of openness and honesty becomes habitual, and we cease to practice any confession. At this point, we tend to separate ourselves from the church. It becomes uncomfortable to be around strong Christians. We fear judgment by God or by members of our spiritual family, so we withdraw. We begin the inexorable process of drifting, the end result of which will be to lose our salvation. Let this not be!

Even after years of honest living, a drifting Christian can slip into a double life, rationalizing secret sin and compromising themself. We tell ourselves, *"I can deal with it."* But the sin gradually hardens our hearts. The spirit in our hearts is slowly starved as we fail to feed it through prayer and Bible study. We become even weaker spiritually while our sinful nature grows stronger. Temptations from our past lives grow more compelling. The crunch of time affects our priorities, as Jesus becomes one of many things in our lives. Church attendance falters, revealing the condition of our hearts. Marriage and other relationships suffer because of the lack of spiritual strength and guidance. Meanwhile our faith plummets. We no longer see the hand of God in our lives. The miracles and victories that fueled our faith in the beginning dwindle to nothing. Those great stories of how we changed radically and overcame challenges slowly decline, and the astonishing things that were happening no longer occur. When drifting, we lose our feelings of gratitude, excitement and joy. Worship no longer thrills our hearts, and we stop being moved by songs and praise. Sermons are no longer effective. We cease talking about our faith and love for God. The farther we drift, the farther away he seems and the more impossible the Christian life appears to be.

Hopefully someone brings you a word of encouragement before you are too far gone! As older Christians, we are eternally grateful for the brothers and sisters who call us back. Whether it was by rebuke or encouragement, we thank God for those who turned us around and woke us up to our drift! We Christians must remain solidly anchored in Jesus or we will get carried away by Satan. We have all seen too many friends carried off by the enemy. We must heed the solemn warning: "For since the message spoken through angels was binding, and every violation and disobedience received its just punishment, how shall we escape if we ignore so great a salvation?" The answer is that we will not escape.

The Jews believed that God delivered his word via messengers/angels and that to ignore or rebel against them brought about swift punishment. In Deuteronomy 33:2 it says that "myriads of holy ones" were present when Moses gave the law of God. The angels were the legal witnesses to God's deliverance of the law. There is a connection between the first paragraph in chapter 2 and the opening paragraph of chapter 1 as the argument returns to how important it is to listen to Jesus. How foolish it would be to ignore God's prophets and probably worse to ignore his angels. The author argues that we are much guiltier if we ignore God's Son, who is his exact representation. He mentions two types of disobedience: *parabasis*, which is a violation or purposefully acting out in rebellion; and *parakoe*, which is imperfect or careless hearing or unwillingness to hear.

Sometimes we knowingly choose to do evil and, of course, that is very bad. We all have a rebellious streak in us, some of us much more than others. Some of us were quietly rebellious when we were younger, seeming good on the outside but full of sin on the inside. Others were in-your-face rebellious. Some of us are fully aware of our sin, while others of us are self-deceived and blame others for our wrongdoing, believing our own propaganda about why we sinned and seeing ourselves as victims instead of sinners.

But oftentimes Christians simply do not pay enough attention to their salvation. We stop listening. We do not willfully sin so much, but we choose not to listen to God's words, hoping that ignorance is an excuse. We all know that it is not. Try that one with the police officer who pulls you over. "I didn't know it was against the law." Try telling that to God! We tend to get comfortable in doing the basics and forget that we are in a struggle between good and evil, light and darkness. We think *"I'm fine"* and drift unwittingly away from our salvation. We hear sermons and think, *"I've heard that before."* We can lose our sense of discovery and slip into routine and tradition. We can sing songs and be numb to the words we are saying. We can even repeat memorized prayers with words that no longer have meaning. Jesus warned us, quoting Isaiah, "These people honor me with their lips, but their hearts are far from me."

Which are you more prone to? Is your principle tendency *parabasis*—outright rebellion? Or are you more prone to *parakoe*—are you one who tends to simply stop listening carefully to the message that brings salvation? Hopefully you are already paying careful attention to the message. If so, then you will continue to grow in your faith.

The writer of Hebrews gives his audience a couple of added reasons to listen to the message that was delivered to them, just in case they need more. He makes one of the comments that reveal that they are second-generation Christians: they received the gospel, not from Jesus directly, but from those who had it straight from him. He states that it "was confirmed to us by those who heard him." This binding message that we must pay careful attention to was delivered by the apostles. In addition, its inspiration was confirmed by various miracles and gifts of the Holy Spirit. We can assume that the audience of Hebrews are eyewitnesses of some of these miraculous gifts. One of the purposes of the miraculous gifts of the Holy Spirit in the first century was to confirm the inspired message to people who did not yet have the completed New Testament. The point of the writer is this: God himself testified to this message, so we had better pay careful attention to it.

It is at this point that the outline we are using (which is the outline our preacher is apparently also using) becomes just a little tricky to follow. After giving us our first strong exhortation in Hebrews 2:1–4, in Hebrews 2:5–9 the sermon returns to discuss just a bit more the superiority of Jesus over the angels.

> *It is not to angels that he has subjected the world to come, about which we are speaking. But there is a place where someone has testified:*
>
> > *"What is mankind that you are mindful of them,*
> > *a son of man that you care for him?*
> > *You made them a little lower than the angels;*
> > *you crowned them with glory and honor*
> > *and put everything under their feet."*
>
> *In putting everything under them, God left nothing that is not subject to them. Yet at present we do not see everything subject to them. But we do see Jesus, who was made lower than the angels for a little while, now crowned with glory and honor because he suffered death, so that by the grace of God he might taste death for everyone.* (Hebrews 2:5–9)

Again, we have scriptures highlighting the supremacy of Jesus. Psalm 8:4–6 is quoted to demonstrate the condition of mankind. It is important to understand that "son of man" does refer to Jesus here. This title was another Hebrew way of saying "man." As our Jewish Christian audience would know, Ezekiel is called "son of man" more than eighty times. Daniel is also called "son of man" (Daniel 8:17), as are others. Jesus, of course, was called Son of Man, but when this was done it was to emphasize his humanness. Jesus is human (Son of Man) and God (Son of God). The psalmist reveals that God made human beings temporarily lower than the angels. This is our current status, as long as we are on the earth in these temporary physical bodies. Nevertheless, God cares for humankind greatly and has subjected all things here on the earth to our rule.

Unfortunately, we see also that on this earth, God's will is not always done (Matthew 6:10), and humans are not the only controlling influence here, as to some extent this is Satan's realm.

But this is not the main point. What the author is telling us here is intended to encourage us greatly. Here is the most spectacular, joy-producing news: Jesus allowed himself to be made "a little lower than the angels." Actually, the NIV does not give the best sense of this passage. The Greek reflects that he was made lower than the angels for just a little while. Jesus became lower than the angels, not in importance, but in power. What a superb concept! Jesus lowered himself to become human so as to save us humans. This is what a good high priest does. It is also the subject of the next section of the book. Jesus came down to a world full of slaves to sin, making himself in the form of a slave, so that he could save us from our hopeless condition. Here is the rest of the incredible news: after making himself lower than the angels, he has been exalted on high by God and is now crowned with glory and honor in the heavens. As Paul put it regarding Christ Jesus:

> *Who, being in very nature God,*
> *did not consider equality with God something to be*
> *used to his own advantage;*
> *rather, he made himself nothing*
> *by taking the very nature of a servant,*
> *being made in human likeness.*
> *And being found in appearance as a man,*
> *he humbled himself*
> *by becoming obedient to death—*
> *even death on a cross!*
> *Therefore God exalted him to the highest place*
> *and gave him the name that is above every name.*
> (Philippians 2:6–9)

Added to this, he will lift us up after the last days so that we will be over the angels. In fact, we will judge angels (1 Corinthians 6:3). This is the Jesus who intercedes for us.

Chapter 4

Jesus Is a Perfect Priest
Hebrews 2:10–18

We now turn to the third sense in which Jesus is far superior to something that the Jews thought was pretty great. Jesus is greater than the prophets. He is much superior to the angels. He is also a perfect high priest.

In bringing many sons and daughters to glory, it was fitting that God, for whom and through whom everything exists, should make the pioneer of their salvation perfect through what he suffered. Both the one who makes people holy and those who are made holy are of the same family. So Jesus is not ashamed to call them brothers and sisters. He says,

"I will declare your name to my brothers and sisters;
in the assembly I will sing your praises." [Psalm 22:22]

And again,
"I will put my trust in him." [Isaiah 8:17]

And again he says,
"Here am I, and the children God has given me." [Isaiah 8:18]

Since the children have flesh and blood, he too shared in their humanity so that by his death he might break the power of him who holds the power of death—that is, the devil—and free those who all their lives were held in slavery by their fear of death. For surely it is not angels he helps, but Abraham's descendants. For this reason he had to be made like them, fully human in every way, in order that he might become a merciful and faithful high priest in service to God, and that he might make atonement for the sins of the people. Because he himself suffered when he was tempted, he is able to help those who are being tempted. (Hebrews 2:10–18)

We find here a powerful argument clarifying the nature and purpose of Jesus. The radical idea is presented that God would "perfect" the Messiah Jesus. This implies that he was not perfect yet! This is one of those words we told you to watch out for. The word "perfect" here is the Greek *teleioo*. It is often, as here, translated as "perfect," but the meaning of the word includes the idea of being mature or fully developed—complete. The word *teleioo* does not normally imply the English idea of "flawless." There is a tremendous depth in the terminology here. This word "perfect" is the same word used in the Pentateuch of the Hebrew Scriptures for consecrating, ordaining and appointing the high priest for service in the tabernacle (Exodus 29:9, 29, 33, 35; Leviticus 4:5, 8:33, 16:32, 21:10; Numbers 3:3). This was required by the law in order for someone to serve in their priestly duties. Of course, it was also required for Jesus to serve as our high priest.

What is astounding is that Jesus was fully perfected by suffering. This idea is radical in light of the views in pagan religions. Even in Judaism, that God would suffer in any way is surprising. That he would suffer for *us* is absolutely mind-boggling. He was made perfect because he endured human suffering and knew what it felt like. He could relate to our struggles because he went through them as well. The suffering that all of us endure in this fallen world he understands! He is called the *archegos*, the "pioneer" or champion of our faith. He is a pioneer in the sense that he led the way for us. He was perfected/completed by resisting temptation and suffering without once sinning—not even a single time. He therefore left a path before us to follow him. When a rich person says to a poor person, "I understand your hardship," it is extremely hard for the poor person to believe that. Billionaire Paul Getty was once quoted as saying, "If you want to be rich like me, you must rise early every morning, work very hard every day, and strike oil." We are tempted to reply, "Whatever you say, Paul." When politicians claim to be able to relate to the common people, most scoff at that. How could they? A poor person suffers many things that people with money will never fathom. But when a rich person comes from poverty, they have instant credibility; in this understanding they become members of a unique community. <u>By suffering, Jesus became a member of the community of those who suffer in this world, and that is all of us.</u> In a real sense, he became family. No wonder the writer says, "Both the one who makes people holy and those who are made holy are of the same family." What a beautiful concept. You are part of Jesus' family because he suffered like you in every way.

Once many years ago, my wife and I (Robert) were asked to do a marriage workshop in Boston titled Radical Love. During one of our main classes, Michele shared about the challenges of life with a chronic illness. She talked about how her illness caused her to miss meetings and how subsequently people in the Church questioned her commitment level. She shared about the challenge of living with pain and being judged as less "giving." The class concluded, and I was surrounded by several men who thanked me and shared additional thoughts on our topic. When I looked over to my wife, I was amazed to see her surrounded by dozens of women. She was an instant hero to them because of what she had suffered—she was relatable as a leader. Jesus understands us because he was one of us. "He too shared in [our] humanity." Jesus was perfect because he also dealt with pain and loss in a way that God the Father and Creator of the heavens did not. God the Father sent us Jesus, Emmanuel, God with us!

Jesus is not the boss, working in an air-conditioned office, looking down on the workers on the factory floor. He came out of his office and is sweating right along with us on the factory floor. We could not go to God, so God came to us. We could not understand God, but God came here so that he could understand us and we could understand him. What a beautiful thing this is!

In verse 17 we read that Jesus was made "fully human." This is an outrageous concept when we consider who God is. Yet how great is this fact. When we sin or when we suffer, our natural desire is to speak to someone who can relate. Nobody wants to share their guilt or suffering with someone who does not "get it" and cannot empathize. Rather, we seek someone who has also suffered and so can identify with our sorrow. Even in the area of sin, we want someone who knows how hard it is to overcome sin, not someone who stands in cold judgment. Jesus knows how hard it is, and that he was successful! About the purpose of Jesus' actions, we read, "...that he might become a merciful and faithful high priest in service to God." Mercy is incredibly important to us who know we are sinners. In order to save us, Jesus had to be full of mercy and faithful in the sense that he would neither despair nor give up on helping us. He was and continues to be our *archegos,* our champion! In ancient times wealthy people could have a champion do battle for them—someone who would fight for their honor, their name or even their life. Jesus is our champion. William Lane in his commentary on Hebrews states about the term "champion" that "the tradition provided the prophets with the basis for developing the significant theological motif of God as the champion of Israel."[3] He is our archegos, our trail blazer who loves us and considers us family. Everyone wants to succeed. We seek mentoring from those who have been successful in an area of importance to us. We hire and pay for professionals who have excelled in their field. We understand that someone cannot show us the way unless they have walked it and distinguished themselves in it. Would you go to a flabby fitness trainer? Jesus was successful in all things. More than that, he was victorious, even over our greatest foe, death itself! Therefore, there is no excuse not to follow Jesus and every reason to focus on him and walk in his steps.

> *The LORD will march out like a champion,*
> *like a warrior he will stir up his zeal;*
> *with a shout he will raise the battle cry*
> *and will triumph over his enemies.* (Isaiah 42:13)

End Notes _____

3. William. L. Lane, *Hebrews 1–8*, Word Biblical Commentary vol. 47a (Dallas: Word Incorporated, 1998), 62.

Chapter 5

Jesus Is Greater Than Moses
Hebrews 3:1–6

In chapters 1 and 2 we have seen the superiority of Jesus over the prophets and the angels. Now in verses 1–6 of chapter 3, we are presented with a comparison of Jesus and Moses. We will see that Jesus is much greater.

> *Therefore, holy brothers and sisters, who share in the heavenly calling, fix your thoughts on Jesus, whom we acknowledge as our apostle and high priest. He was faithful to the one who appointed him, just as Moses was faithful in all God's house. Jesus has been found worthy of greater honor than Moses, just as the builder of a house has greater honor than the house itself. For every house is built by someone, but God is the builder of everything. "Moses was faithful as a servant in all God's house," bearing witness to what would be spoken by God in the future. But Christ is faithful as the Son over God's house. And we are his house, if indeed we hold firmly to our confidence and the hope in which we glory.*
> (Hebrews 3:1–6)

We will look at what makes Jesus superior to Moses, but first, let us notice that we are addressed as "holy" brothers and sisters. This formal address would have normally been applied only to the Jews who kept God's law. The writer is reminding us that now the holy ones of God are Jesus' people, whether Jew or Gentile. The word "holy" implies that someone or something has been specially set apart to do God's will, like the instruments of the tabernacle or temple that could be used only for holy purposes such as for sacrifice and worship. Like them, we have been made unique and have been set apart for sacred use. We are vessels for noble purposes (2 Timothy 2:20). We are not ordinary citizens; we share a great responsibility to fulfill our one purpose, to carry out God's will. This purpose and responsibility cannot be set aside lightly.

In the first verse we find the command to "fix" our thoughts on Jesus. This is not a call to passively consider Jesus' life. It is a command to focus our mental energy, to come to a full understanding of how splendid Jesus is, and to make a great effort to become like him. The Greek word here is *katanoein,* which means to consider, ponder, meditate on, or look on with a concentrated gaze. There are so many things in life that are demanding our attention that it is difficult to be focused on anything for an extended period of time. The twenty-first century is the age of distraction. With the internet, laptops, tablets and smartphones, we have entertainment, information, news, communication and masses of trivial data pushed before our eyes, constantly available at our fingertips anytime, anywhere. It is difficult even for the strong to resist the temptation to be drawn in and consumed by our electronics. It is far too easy to passively absorb entertainment rather than having a focused quiet time with God. When we are troubled, we have the option to simply escape into the cyberworld, watching a screen rather than focusing on Jesus.

I (Robert) once heard a sermon by my good friend Mike Taliaferro in which he shared the example of being in a theater in Brazil when the screen was out of focus, so the crowd began chanting "Focus, focus." His point was how the heavens must so often be shouting the same to us Christians: "Focus, focus," as we walk through our days, good and bad. The center of creation is Jesus, and the power of a victorious life comes from Jesus! He is the inspiration and the example. We cannot live a godly life with any measure of success without a strong connection to him. When people lose sight of Jesus, they lose their vital connection with their "apostle" whom God sent to us and the "high priest" who stands before God on our behalf. It is from him that we receive the power and motivation to overcome obstacles, to find victory in defeat and to excel in God. He is the way, the truth and the life! The challenge of this century is to keep our minds laser focused on him.

Unlike the movie theater illustration above, a lack of focus on Jesus can be subtle and go undetected for years. Like a rechargeable battery that will not fully charge because its chemicals have decomposed, is a person's faith who lacks focus. Unfocused Christians hang on to their faith and continue their traditions but are overcome by their temptations and hobble through poor relationships and bad marriages, eventually falling for the same temptations as their non-Christian neighbors. This is a trap that cripples millions who are professing the power of God that comes from the Christian life, yet who are living powerlessly. It is why so many people in our world today see "Christians" as no different from members of any other religion. Because of their weak connection brought on by a lack of focus on Christ, they are barely different from everyone else. Jesus is part of their life; but in reality he must be the center of our lives in order for us to have life to the full. How well focused has your vision of Christ been this week, this month, this year or this decade?

Sometimes, what challenges our focus is not a worldly distraction. Sometimes, even spiritual topics can be a distraction from Jesus. It is easy for even the strong to get caught up in the different aspects of the Christian life. Christians strive to improve discipline, increase Bible knowledge, improve in righteousness and become more effective. To be sure, all these things are important, but they are only aspects of our walk and must be understood and practiced in the context of fixing our spiritual eyes on and following Jesus. Some, in their effort to legitimize their faith, turn religion into a philosophy of self-denial or self-discipline. Others get lost in the pursuit of spiritual "self-fulfillment" and being their "best" or being "blessed." Without a focus on Jesus, the "power of an indestructible life" (Hebrews 7) is a mirage. That power only comes from following Jesus. There are unproductive and unfulfilling versions of Christianity out there because of those who zealously practice religion without Jesus as the center of their lives. They fill churches with people who pretend to be happy and in control but who suffer nearly the same defeats as the rest of the world. They do not know the power of the Christian life because they do not know the real Christ, Jesus. He is the "cornerstone" by which everything should be aligned and measured (1 Peter 2:7). He is the "foundation" on which we should build our lives (1 Corinthians 3:11). Religion is only right when it is in line with Jesus. Therefore, let us focus our thoughts on him.

In verse 2 Jesus is proclaimed as the faithful one even as Moses was faithful. Moses is the hero and founder of Judaism. He is the great lawgiver from whom Judaism receives its identity. To hear that one much greater than Moses had come to Israel would be fighting words for most Jews, yet Jesus is presented here as greatly superior to Moses. N.T. Wright describes the relationship between Moses and Jesus as not so much a rivalry, but rather as a local high school team versus a nationally ranked professional team. If a person supports his local team, it does not mean he will not also support the professional-level team. But between the two, there is no competition.

Moses and Jesus are both heroes but are not in the same league!

It is inspiring to consider the fact that Moses and Jesus are miraculously similar to one another and at the same time Jesus is infinitely greater than Moses. How did God manage to make both of these true? God told Moses that he would raise up one similar to him.

> The LORD said to me: "What you say is good. I will raise up for them a prophet like you from among their fellow Israelites, and I will put my words in his mouth. He will tell them everything I command him. I myself will call to account anyone who does not listen to my words that the prophet speaks in my name." (Deuteronomy 18:17–19)

Here we see the admonition, fifteen centuries before Hebrews was written, that we had better fix our thoughts on Jesus. Consider both the ways that Jesus is like Moses and, at the same time, is far greater than Moses. Truly Moses is the type and Jesus is the antitype!

1. **Pharaoh had the wild premonition that a Jewish baby would replace him on his throne. He did not know which Jewish boy to kill, so he decided to kill all the Jewish boy babies. Yet God saved Moses from Pharaoh. Similarly, King Herod had a seemingly unreasonable premonition that a Jewish baby would replace him on his throne. He did not know which Jewish boy to kill, so he decided to kill all the Jewish boy babies from the region around Bethlehem. Yet God saved Jesus from Herod.**

2. **God's people were enslaved. God sent a savior to free his people from captivity. The first time he did this, the savior was Moses; the second time it was Jesus.**

3. **Moses left the palace, where he was at the right hand of Pharaoh, so that he could deliver God's people. Jesus left heaven, where he was at the right hand of the Father, so that he could deliver God's people (Philippians 2:6–7).**

4. **God called Moses out of Egypt so that he could save his people. God called Jesus out of Egypt so that he could save his people (Hosea 11:1: "Out of Egypt I called my son").**

5. **Moses went out into the desert for forty years to prepare for his**

ministry to save God's people. Jesus went out into the desert for forty days to prepare for his ministry to save God's people. But then, he is Jesus.

6. Aaron spoke, preparing the way for Moses. John the Baptist spoke, preparing the way for Jesus.

7. Israel was baptized into Moses in the Red Sea, at which point they left Egypt and slavery. We are baptized into Christ, at which point we leave behind the world and our slavery to sin (1 Corinthians 10:1–2).

8. God spoke to Moses on Mt. Sinai. God spoke to Jesus on the Mount of Transfiguration, and guess who was there with him: Moses!

Truly, Jesus is like Moses, but consider the ways that Jesus is greatly superior in status than Moses:

1. Moses saved physical Israel from physical slavery in physical Egypt. Jesus saves spiritual Israel from spiritual slavery in spiritual Egypt. The first effect is temporary, the second eternal.

2. Moses received the law. Jesus is the law.

3. Moses gave them bread that kept Israel alive physically (actually, God gave them bread). Jesus is the bread of heaven that keeps us alive spiritually and that gives us eternal life (John 6:25–59).

4. Moses gave them water (actually, God gave them water). Jesus gives the water that wells up to eternal life—the Holy Spirit (John 7:37–39, 4:14).

5. Moses was a servant in God's house (Numbers 12:6–7; Hebrews 3:5). Jesus built God's house (Hebrews 3:3).

6. Moses was faithful in all God's house (Numbers 12:7), but Jesus is faithful over God's house (Hebrews 3:6).

God is telling the Jews that, no matter how great Moses was—and he was truly great—it is time to give our attention to the one of whom he was merely a type. Let us fix our eyes on—let us give our full attention to—the antitype, Jesus.

In Hebrews 3:6 God makes it clear that our being part of God's family or "house"—a very Jewish point of pride and identity—depends entirely on remaining faithful to Jesus until the end. Abandon Jesus and you lose everything! Let us decide right here and now that we will fix our thoughts on Jesus, the pioneer and perfecter of our faith.

Chapter 6

Exhortation #2: Make Every Effort
Hebrews 3:7–4:13

W
e are about to receive our second of the five great admonitions in Hebrews. Really, it is both a warning and an admonition. We are warned against falling into unbelief (Hebrews 3:7–19) and are admonished to make every effort to enter the promised eternal rest (Hebrews 4:1–13).

> *So, as the Holy Spirit says:*
>
> *"Today, if you hear his voice,*
> *do not harden your hearts*
> *as you did in the rebellion,*
> *during the time of testing in the wilderness,*
> *where your ancestors tested and tried me,*
> *though for forty years they saw what I did.*
> *That is why I was angry with that generation;*
> *I said, 'Their hearts are always going astray,*
> *and they have not known my ways.'*
> *So I declared on oath in my anger,*
> *'They shall never enter my rest.'"*
>
> *See to it, brothers and sisters, that none of you has a sinful, unbelieving heart that turns away from the living God. But encourage one another daily, as long as it is called "Today," so that none of you may be hardened by sin's deceitfulness. We have come to share in Christ, if indeed we hold our original conviction firmly to the very end. As has just been said:*
>
> *"Today, if you hear his voice,*
> *do not harden your hearts*
> *as you did in the rebellion."* (Hebrews 3:7–15)

To issue this stern warning from God, the writer uses Psalm 95 to create an analogy from the history of God's people: their escape from slavery in

Egypt, their wandering in the wilderness for forty years, and their eventual entrance into the promised land. In this extended metaphor, our life as Christians is compared to the generation that left Egypt and wandered in the desert.[4] There are several comparisons to be drawn. Like Israel, all of us were at one time enslaved in our own spiritual Egypt due to our sins. Just as Moses set God's people free, we have been freed from our spiritual bondage by the second Moses, Jesus. We too are being tested in the desert. We too are holding on to the hope of entering our eternal rest in the promised land. The Christian life is a long journey with many tests and periods of trial. The original recipients of this letter were going through their time of testing as well, as they faced great difficulties. Renewed persecution lay ahead. Despite the fact that most of us reading this will never face the same level of challenges as the early Hebrew Christians did, we do have our challenges as we encounter many trials and temptations in life. There is a suggestion in this section that we could end up like those who wandered in the wasteland. We may be rescued from our life of sin, but we may fall in a desert and never enter the promised land. This is the warning of Hebrews 3:7–4:11.

Foreshadows from the Time of Moses Fulfilled in the Christian Life	
Old Testament Foreshadow	*New Testament Equivalent*
Slavery in Egypt	Slavery to sin (before baptism)
Wandering in the desert	Life of a disciple of Jesus
Entering the promised land	Entering heaven

The Christian life is an all-or-nothing proposition. We cannot live it halfheartedly and still experience its great victories and benefits. We are warned not to harden our hearts during the time of testing. When we are tested, we are usually tempted to despair or get angry at God. Sometimes we even question God. It is difficult to stay faithful to the end, but it is a requirement for our ultimate salvation (3:14). How do you respond when times are difficult? What is your attitude toward God when things go wrong? How do you handle suffering as a Christian? The answers to these questions reveal our level of faith and commitment to God. Victory always comes at the end of the trial if we stay faithful to the end, but if we give in to despair or quit, we rob ourselves of the victories that lie ahead of us.

The Hebrews rescued from Egypt grew impatient and angry, and ultimately judged God. They judged him unfairly, because they could not see his long-term plan and chose not to trust his promises. It was a great tragedy that despite seeing so many miracles they still doubted him. In many ways, faith is the greatest determinant of a person's failure or success in life. A person may have very few possessions, but with great faith, that little can turn into great blessings. Another person may start out with a lot of blessings, but because of having little faith they can lose everything. Faith reveals what is most important and what really matters to a person. Most everyone seeks riches, believing that riches will bring them happiness. Although we know better, it is still difficult to think and live otherwise. On the other hand, faith brings contentment, but it can also be a painful road with many struggles. Faith gives the strength necessary to go all the way to victory. Without it, there is no way to succeed in life with all its challenges.

Jesus spent much of his time teaching his followers to be men and women of faith—to trust in him as they trusted in God. Many parables and situations were lessons about a faith that trusts the Father despite hardship. There were the five thousand and four thousand that needed to be fed, and yet the twelve and seven basketfuls of leftovers the apostles collected. There was the great storm and Jesus walking to them on the water. Just as Jesus warned that we are not to judge each other too quickly (Matthew 7:1–2), Paul warned to not judge situations before the appointed time (1 Corinthians 4:5). God works for our benefit always. That does not mean he removes the obstacles or the suffering from our path. Our world is cursed and fallen. Therefore, we can expect to have troubles and hardships. This will especially be the case when we set out to do right and live right. God is able to work in any situation, no matter how hard or impossible it may seem, but everything depends on faith. The Father works through time and rarely on our schedule. We must always be patient and trust in him. Our need to rely on God and trust his timing in spite of appearances is illustrated by the following:

The Woodcutter's Wisdom

Once there was an old man who lived in a tiny village. Although poor, he was envied by all, for he owned a beautiful horse. Even the king coveted his treasure. A horse like this had never been seen before—such was its splendor, its majesty, its strength. People offered fabulous prices for the steed, but the old man always refused.

One morning he found that the horse was not in the stable. All the village came to see him. "You old fool," they scoffed, "we told you that someone would steal your horse. We warned you that you would be robbed. You are so poor. How could you ever hope to protect such a valuable animal? It would have been better to have sold him. You could have gotten whatever price you wanted. No amount would have been too high. Now the horse is gone, and you've been cursed with misfortune."

The old man responded, "Don't speak too quickly. Say only that the horse is not in the stable. That is all we know; the rest is judgment. Whether I have been cursed or not, how can you know? How can you judge?"

The people of the village laughed. They thought that the man was crazy. They had always thought he was a fool; if he was not, he would have sold the horse and lived off the money.

After fifteen days, the horse returned. He had not been stolen; he had run away into the forest. Not only had he returned, he had brought a dozen wild horses with him. Once again the village people gathered around the woodcutter and spoke. "Old man, you were right and we were wrong. What we thought was a curse was a blessing. Please forgive us."

The man responded, "Once again, you go too far. Say only that the horse is back. State only that a dozen horses returned with him, but don't judge. How do you know if this is a blessing or not?"

The old man had a son, an only son. The young man began to break the wild horses. After a few days, he fell from one of the horses and broke both legs. Once again the villagers gathered around the old man and cast their judgments.

"You were right," they said. "You have been proved right. The dozen horses were not a blessing. They were a curse. Your only son has broken his legs, and now in your old age you have no one to help you. Now you are poorer than ever."

The old man spoke again. "You people are obsessed with judging. Don't go so far. Say only that my son broke his legs. Who knows if it is a blessing or a curse?"

It so happened that a few weeks later the country engaged

in war against a neighboring country. All the young men of the village were required to join the army. Only the son of the old man was excluded, because he was injured. Once again the people gathered around the old man, crying and screaming because their sons had been taken.

"You were right, old man," they wept. "God knows you were right. This proves it. Yours son's accident was a blessing. His legs may be broken, but at least he is with you. Our sons are gone forever."

The old man spoke again. "It is impossible to talk with you. You always draw conclusions. No one knows. Say only this: Your sons had to go to war, and mine did not. No one knows if it is a blessing or a curse. No one is wise enough to know. Only God knows."

In Hebrews 3:7–15 we learn that the onus of staying faithful—of not hardening our hearts—is put on us as a body. We are to "see to it" that none of us has a hard heart. If we are going to make it, we will need to give to and receive from one another plenty of encouragement. We cannot do this alone. We are our brothers' and sisters' keepers. How much and how often do we need encouragement in order to keep walking by faith? As long as it is called "Today." As far as we know, it is always called today.

> *Who were they who heard and rebelled? Were they not all those Moses led out of Egypt? And with whom was he angry for forty years? Was it not with those who sinned, whose bodies perished in the wilderness? And to whom did God swear that they would never enter his rest if not to those who disobeyed? So we see that they were not able to enter, because of their unbelief.* (Hebrews 3:16–19)

The warning from God's perspective is brought home with the stern admonition that just because someone is chosen does not mean that they are guaranteed a place with him. The great majority in the evangelical Christian world today believe that once we are saved, we can never lose our inheritance with God. This is the doctrine sometimes called "once saved, always saved" that we introduced earlier. The Hebrew writer makes it crystal clear in many statements that this is simply not the case. As was already said of verse 14, we will come to share in Christ only if we hold to our original commitment. The converse is this: if we do not hold our original confession of Christ firmly to the end, we will not share in him. Unbelief can cause anyone to lose their place with God. Verses 16 through 19 compare those who do not make it in the Christian life with those who died in the desert because of their lack of faith. It is made clear that this can happen to any of us as well if we fall into "unbelief" in God's promises and power. Think about it. Meditate on this picture. Of those who left Egypt and were saved by passing through the Red Sea and being baptized into Moses, how many of them made it to the promised land? The answer: not many! This is a stark warning to us, and we had better pay attention.

From James 2:14-26 we learn that a genuine, saving faith is a working faith. From Hebrews we learn that a genuine, saving faith is a persistent faith. We also learn that a saving faith is an obedient faith. Notice that both in Hebrews 3:18–19 and in Hebrews 4:2, faith and obedience are treated as synonyms. Were they not able to enter because of their disobedience (v. 18) or because of their lack of faith (v. 19)? The answer is yes! These are two sides of the same coin. If we are to make it to the promised land, we must continue to walk by faith—an obedient faith.

If this warning were the whole story, we would be left discouraged, would we not? Fortunately, God follows up the stern warning to watch our heart with an admonition concerning what we can do so that we do not "fall in the desert," so that we can be sure we will enter final rest in heaven. Praise God for that!

> Therefore, since the promise of entering his rest still stands, let us be careful that none of you be found to have fallen short of it. For we also have had the good news proclaimed to us, just as they did; but the message they heard was of no value to them, because they did not share the faith of those who obeyed. Now we who have believed enter that rest, just as God has said,
>
> > "So I declared on oath in my anger,
> > 'They shall never enter my rest.'"
>
> And yet his works have been finished since the creation of the world. For somewhere he has spoken about the seventh day in these words: "On the seventh day God rested from all

his works." And again in the passage above he says, "They shall never enter my rest."

Therefore since it still remains for some to enter that rest, and since those who formerly had the good news proclaimed to them did not go in because of their disobedience, God again set a certain day, calling it "Today." This he did when a long time later he spoke through David, as in the passage already quoted:

> *"Today, if you hear his voice,*
> *do not harden your hearts."*

For if Joshua had given them rest, God would not have spoken later about another day. There remains, then, a Sabbath-rest for the people of God; for anyone who enters God's rest also rests from their works, just as God did from his. Let us, therefore, make every effort to enter that rest, so that no one will perish by following their example of disobedience. (Hebrews 4:1–11)

In this section we have a summary and a comment on the second warning. This section is very emotional. The writer is pleading with us to keep hold of God's promises. He begins with the reminder that this promise still stands and therefore we must hold on and not be found falling short. The word for "let us be careful" is *phobethomen*, which means "let us be afraid." The irony lies in that after being told many times not to give in to fear, but rather to be faithful, now we are told what to be afraid of. Our fear should be of being found faithless and missing the promise. The writer reminds us that we have the same God and similar promises to those the Jews had as they wandered in the desert. As they hoped to enter the promised land, we hope to enter heaven. We should be like Joshua and Caleb, who never doubted God and were the only ones of their generation who entered the promised land. It was said of Caleb: "But because my servant Caleb has a different spirit and follows me wholeheartedly, I will bring him into the land he went to, and his descendants will inherit it" (Numbers 14:24).

Joshua and Caleb trusted God. When the negative and fearful report came back from the other ten who spied out the promise land, Joshua and Caleb wanted to enter despite potential opposition, as they trusted God. They were the ones who obeyed the Lord. Obedience from the heart is always born from faith. Fear is the enemy of faith. It drives faith out of the heart. A heart filled with fear cannot muster the courage or strength necessary to obey God, especially in tough times. We should not fear what the world can do to us. Whom should we fear? "But I will show you whom you should fear: Fear him who, after your body has been killed, has authority to throw you into hell. Yes, I tell you, fear him. (Luke 12:5) The only one we should fear is God. God's message must be heard with faith or else it sounds unreasonable, even impossible.

The end of the long and arduous journey of the Hebrews was rest in the promised land. But this required maintaining faith along the way. It also required making every effort. Without faith, neither they nor we will ever enter God's eternal rest. Again, we are warned from Psalm 95 not to let our hearts be hardened. We are reminded that we must keep our hearts soft and open to God. We are reminded that he will not grant rest to the unbelieving.

But God does have a wonderful and long-anticipated rest in store for us. "There remains then, a Sabbath-rest for the people of God" (v. 9). When we enter into God's rest we will rest from our work (v. 10). We have a great reward that God has prepared for us. Oh, it is worth it. Can you feel that finish line? How will we make it? How will we enter?

In verse 11 we have the second exhortation summed up in this: "Let us, therefore, make every effort to enter that rest." How will we make it to our promised land—to the place where God has an eternal rest in store for us? We need to make every effort. How hard should we work to serve God? As hard as we can. Is this works salvation? No, it is the works that are motivated by our salvation, because we are already saved. We love because he loved us—Christ's love compels us (2 Corinthians 5:14). We can never rest on our laurels; there is no Christian vacation. Joshua did not give Israel rest. Neither can we rest until our Christian walk is done. We cannot stop being spiritual or relying on God. Our journey is not over until it is over. We look so forward to that day when God will say to us, "Well done, good and faithful servant.... Come and share your master's happiness!" (Matthew 25:23). Can you picture that day right now? Can you feel God saying to you "well done"? Brothers and sisters, that day is not yet here, so let us keep walking in an obedient faith, and let us make every effort. If we do, we can be assured that our day of rest will come. What a day that will be!

For the word of God is alive and active. Sharper than any

double-edged sword, it penetrates even to dividing soul and spirit, joints and marrow; it judges the thoughts and attitudes of the heart. Nothing in all creation is hidden from God's sight. Everything is uncovered and laid bare before the eyes of him to whom we must give account. (Hebrews 4:12–13)

The close of this argument about faith and rest ends with a final comment about God's word. The Jewish Christian audience of Hebrews know that the word of God is sacred and must be obeyed no matter what. Perhaps they could question the validity of the preacher's strong admonitions concerning their lives, but no one could doubt the word of God. The arguments made in the book of Hebrews are supported by heavy reliance on the Old Testament. None can doubt what happened to God's people who disobeyed in the wilderness. The writer makes it clear to his hearers that the warnings and admonitions are not his own but come directly from the sacred text. If they have a problem it is with God and his word, not with the one preaching to them. He reminds them that the pain they feel is because the Word is like a sword that cuts. He reminds them that we shall all be judged by it. We are reminded that we will all have to give an account for our decisions and actions. These are powerful reminders!

Let us summarize our second admonition. How can we be assured of our salvation—of entering our promised rest with God?

1. Let us give to and receive from our fellow wanderers in the desert all the encouragement we can (Hebrews 3:12–13).

2. Live a life of faith and obedience (Hebrews 3:16-19, 4:6)

3. Fear the right thing! Let us have a healthy fear of falling short (Hebrews 4:1–2).

4. Do not stop. Do not rest. Keep on walking. Make every effort (Hebrews 4:8-11).

5. Let God's word do its work. Listen to it. Let it affect you (Hebrews 4:12–13).

End Notes _____

4. This metaphor is also used in Jude 5 and 1 Corinthians 10:1–12.

Chapter 7

Jesus Is Greater Than the High Priest
Hebrews 4:14–5:10

> *Therefore, since we have a great high priest who has ascended into heaven, Jesus the Son of God, let us hold firmly to the faith we profess. For we do not have a high priest who is unable to empathize with our weaknesses, but we have one who has been tempted in every way, just as we are—yet he did not sin.* (Hebrews 4:14–15)

This section is a continuation of the thoughts begun in Hebrews 2:10–18 concerning the ministry and priesthood of our savior Jesus Christ. The point the Hebrew writer is making is that Jesus is a vastly superior high priest to those who took the role among the Jews. In fact, Jesus is not just superior—he is a perfect high priest for us. And what a high priest he is! We will talk about the high priest in a moment, but first let us consider the role of a priest generally in all religions, and more specifically in Judaism.

What is the role of a priest? In the Near East, the role of a priest was to represent the people to the gods. The word in Latin for priest is *pontifex*, which literally means bridge maker. The priest was a bridge connecting the people with the gods. The priest or priestess was to make sacrifices in the name of the common people or to enact rituals so that the people could be blessed by the gods. The ideal priest would know the language of the people and also the "language" of the gods. The Jews, of course, had their priests as well, and their role among the Jewish people was similar to that of priests among the pagans (with the difference, of course, that they communicated with a real God!). They were of the tribe of Levi and, more specifically, were descendants of Aaron. In Judaism, the priest was the go-between who represented the people to Yahweh. So, the priest is a bridge, a connection, a mediator, a go-between. For us as humans, a priest is a means of communicating to one who is much greater than ourselves. He is a means of giving praise to God and of seeking blessing from him. The priests were to be devoted in a special way to worshipping God so that the people could give attention to the more mundane activities of life, such as raising crops, trading, making war or pursuing practical industries. It is difficult to be devoted to the things of God and to everyday things at the same time, so the people needed priests to communicate what pertained to God.

We too needed someone to speak to God on our behalf. Such a person should know much of us and much of God—he should be able to speak both the language of God and the language of humans. Surely, many of the sons of Aaron took their role seriously and did a pretty good job. But how much greater a priest is Jesus? Incomparably so! He is indescribably superior to any priest who ever came before him. He certainly knows the things of God quite well, much better than the sons of Aaron did, as he is the Son of God. He can represent God to us far better than any Levite could. After all, he was God in the flesh: "The Word became flesh and made his dwelling among us. We have seen his glory, the glory of the one and only Son, who came from the Father, full of grace and truth" (John 1:14). Jesus know's God's language perfectly well.

But that is not all. Not even close. Not only can he perfectly represent God to us, he can perfectly represent us to God. What makes him such a great priest is that he came down from heaven and took on flesh. He can relate to us; he can empathize with us because he has gone through everything that we go through. The Greek word for empathize here is *sympatheo*. Literally, it means touched with the same feeling. Jesus can feel together with us. He was "tempted in every way, just as we are." What a comfort that is. Have you ever felt that God is too distant from you—that he cannot comprehend the suffering and the temptation you are experiencing? This is certainly how the Greeks felt about their gods. They were far removed from humans. They could not relate to us and we could not relate to them. The priesthood of Jesus is greater than anything the Greeks could even conceive of, but it is also much greater than the priesthood the Jews had.

This is such a blessing to our lives! Remember that you have the perfect priest, Jesus Christ. He definitely can relate to you. You are feeling lonely? Got that one covered. You are feeling tempted to lash out at those hurting you—especially if they are those closest to you, whom you love? Your priest Jesus can totally relate. You want to take a break from your labor, to pull back from battle and just plain rest? Jesus knows what that feels like. He was tempted with that one as strongly as you are. We have a great high priest who has ascended into heaven. He came down and became just like us (except that he did not sin!), but he has now gone back up, where he can perfectly represent your needs, your desires and your longings to the Father. What an amazing priest!

What is the conclusion of the matter? "Let us then approach God's throne of grace with confidence, so that we may receive mercy and find grace to help us in our time of need" (4:16).

Do you have any idea how remarkable this is? Stop for a minute and think about this. If we were inventing a religion out of our own imagination, we could not have dreamed up such a thing. Through our priest Jesus we can approach God's throne with confidence. We can come to the King of the entire universe, the Creator of everything, in full confidence that he will hear us; and he will answer us with mercy and grace. Why? Because we have a priest who can speak to the Father for us. His name is Jesus. The Jews had nothing even remotely like this. To them, Jehovah was a God to be feared and approached with great respect and trepidation, if at all. All of us have had imperfect parents—some worse than others. We came to our father, or perhaps our mother, needing encouragement or comfort or just a shoulder to cry on, but instead our parent was not there or was harsh or unsympathetic. This will NEVER happen when we approach the Father through the Son. We can come with our needs in hand, completely vulnerable, and we can come with confidence. We will be heard, and we will receive mercy. That is the kind of priest we have.

But we are getting carried away here. This section is not just about priests in general, it is specifically about the high priest. What was the role of the high priest in Judaism? It was to make annual atonement for the sins of the people.

> *Every high priest is selected from among the people and is appointed to represent the people in matters related to God, to offer gifts and sacrifices for sins. He is able to deal gently with those who are ignorant and are going astray, since he himself is subject to weakness. This is why he has to offer sacrifices for his own sins, as well as for the sins of the people.* (Hebrews 5:1–3)

As the writer of Hebrews points out for those of us who do not know, the high priest was selected from among the sons of Aaron to take on a special role with a number of responsibilities. For the Jews in Jerusalem at the time of Jesus under the Romans, the high priest had an important political function as well as a religious one. But it is not his political role that is in view here. One of the duties of the high priest, as the writer points out to us, was to offer both gifts and sacrifices at the temple in Jerusalem on a regular basis. We will discuss these gifts and sacrifices when we get to Hebrews 8. For now, let us consider the most important single role that the high priest played, which was on the Day of Atonement, Yom Kippur. It was on this day that atonement was made for the sins of the people so that they could offer worship to Yahweh and so that God could dwell among them and they could be his people. The sins atoned for by the sacrifice on Yom Kippur were those done in ignorance, inadvertent sins—not willful sins. We will discuss this distinction more in later chapters. In any case, the work of the high priest was very important, to say the least.

We will say more about the role of the high priest when we get to chapter 9 of Hebrews, but to simplify, on one day out of the year the high priest went through a carefully scripted ritual. The entire ceremony is outlined in Leviticus 16:3–28. First the high priest washed his hands and feet in the laver. Then he changed into perfectly white robes. Next, he laid his hands on a bull he had paid for and then sacrificed the bull on the altar of sacrifice for his own sins. "Aaron shall bring the bull for his own sin offering to make atonement for himself and his household, and he is to slaughter the bull for his own sin offering" (Leviticus 16:11). The blood of this sacrifice was sprinkled around the holy place, where the shew bread and the menorah were, which is where the other priests also served daily.

Having made atonement for his own sins, the high priest then filled a large censer with incense, lit it on fire, carefully lifted up a corner of the curtain before the holy of holies (or most holy place) and placed the censer inside, according to the instruction, "He is to put the incense on the fire before the Lord and the smoke of the incense will conceal the atonement cover above the tablets of the covenant law, so that he will not die" (Leviticus 16:13). Imagine the scene here. The high priest is about to go into the holy of holies to make atonement for the sins of the people, but first he must fill the room with incense so thick that he cannot see his hand in front of his face. Why? Because otherwise he would see God and die! Do you think that the Jewish high priests felt a sense of fear and dread as they passed behind the curtain? You bet they did.

Now that all was prepared, the high priest then sacrificed a goat as a sin offering for the people and mixed its blood with the bull's blood. Very carefully, he pulled back the curtain into the holy of holies, stepped into the very presence of God, and sprinkled blood from the sacrifice on the mercy seat, which was on top of the ark of the covenant, between the cherubim. "In this way he will make atonement for the most holy place because of the uncleanness and rebellion of the Israelites, whatever their sin has been" (Leviticus 16:16). A tradition developed among the Jews that when the high priest entered the holy of holies, a rope was tied around his ankle. If anything happened to him while he was making atonement for the sins of the people, they would not dare to enter to retrieve his body. They would pull him out by his ankle. Only one day in the year, and only after sacrificing a bull for his own sin and filling the holy of holies with a thick cloud of incense, did the high priest dare to enter the inner sanctum for just a few moments to sprinkle blood on the mercy seat, and even then, only with a rope tied around his ankle.[5]

Contrast this with the ministry of our great and glorious high priest Jesus! Really, there is no comparison, but this is what the Hebrew writer does for us anyway. He contrasts the high priests in the order of Aaron with Jesus. In some ways, Jesus was much like the high priest. Like them, he was "selected from among the people" and represented them in matters relating to God. Therefore he could deal with them gently. The Greek word translated as "deal gently" here is similar to the one translated "mercy" in Hebrews 4:16. It is *metriopatheo,* which literally means to affect moderately. It means to show compassion. This high priest never gets irritated, even if you bug him all the time. He does not get short with you even when your motives are not pure. He does not deal with you as your sins deserve (Psalms 103:10), that is for sure.

But there are more things that make Jesus different as a high priest than there are ways in which he was similar, as the Hebrew writer points out to us.

1. **Unlike the Jewish high priests, he was without sin (Hebrews 4:15, 5:3).**

2. **He serves in a greater tabernacle—the perfect one in heaven (Hebrews 4:14, 9:11).**

3. **He is a priest forever. He does not die and get replaced (Hebrews 5:6).**

4. **He is a priest in the order of Melchizedek, not of Aaron (Hebrews 5:6, 10).**

The Jewish high priests had to offer sacrifices for their own sins (5:3). Not so with Jesus. He could skip the first couple of steps in the Yom Kippur ceremony. And we do not need to hold periodic elections to keep the high priesthood office occupied. Jesus is a priest forever. He does not serve in a sanctuary that wears out and needs occasional repairs, as did the tabernacle and, later, the temple. No, he serves in a perfect, unchanging tabernacle, the heavenly one. We can feel totally confident going to this high priest, can we not?

And by the way, Jesus is not in the order of Aaron. He is in the order of Melchizedek, and that is a much greater order of priests. This will be discussed in great detail after our next little exhortation, and we need this exhortation before we pass on to the subject of Melchizedek.

Despite his exalted position, Jesus is a humble high priest. He did not assume the exalted position on his own. He did not take the honor on himself. It was given to him by his Father, just as Aaron was chosen by God. He was made a priest, he did not appoint himself.

> *And no one takes this honor on himself, but he receives it when called by God, just as Aaron was.*
> *In the same way, Christ did not take on himself the glory of becoming a high priest. But God said to him,*
>> *"You are my Son;*
>>> *today I have become your father."*
> *And he says in another place,*
>> *"You are a priest forever,*
>>> *in the order of Melchizedek."* (Hebrews 5:4–6)

Jesus is serving now as high priest in the heavens, advocating for us in the throne room of God. But he began his priestly ministry while still in the body here. He did the things a high priest ought to do. "During the days of Jesus' life on earth, he offered up prayers and petitions with fervent cries and tears to the one who could save him from death, and he was heard because of his reverent submission" (Hebrews 5:7). In the Garden of Gethsemane Jesus cried in great anguish for his own sake, but as a great high priest would, he submitted himself for our sake to the Father's will, to the point of death, even death on a cross.

Jesus was so humble that, despite possessing the glory of the Son of God, he learned obedience through undergoing suffering: "Son though he was, he learned obedience from what he suffered and, once made perfect, he became the source of eternal salvation for all who obey him" (Hebrews 5:8–9).

He "learned," not in the sense of gaining information about obedience, but in the sense that he experienced the pain and heartbreak that is earned by sinners due to their disobedience. In other words, <u>he learned what it is like for us humans to suffer the consequences of our sins, even though he himself did not sin.</u> He "was numbered with the transgressors" (Isaiah 53:12), even though he is not a transgressor. That is how stupendous a high priest Jesus is. He willingly allowed himself to be considered a sinner and to go through what sinners go through, even though he never sinned. Similarly, Jesus was baptized "to fulfill all righteousness" (Matthew 3:15). In other words, Jesus, as our high priest, experienced all that sinners must experience, including the baptism that we must undergo.

And thus Jesus was made, not only a superior high priest, but a perfect one. He was perfect, not in the sense of being sinless (although Jesus certainly was sinless!). He was perfect (Greek: *teleon*) in the sense of being complete. Before he came in the flesh he had sufficient knowledge of God, of course, but he was not yet complete. He did not know our human "language." A perfect high priest knows the language of God and of those to whom he ministers for God. When Jesus came as a human and suffered all that we suffer through, he became complete as a high priest—perfect in his deity and in his humanity. The result has great implications for us: when Jesus was made complete through suffering, he became the source of salvation for all who obey him. Thank you, priest Jesus! The Hebrew writer sums it up this way: "And [Jesus] was designated by God to be a high priest in the order of Melchizedek" (Hebrews 5:10). Is this Melchizedek guy a bit of a mystery to you? You are not alone. We are about to head into some deep biblical waters here, which is why the writer of Hebrews must first give us our third admonition.

End Notes _____

5. For the sake of simplicity, we are not including the role of the scapegoat in the ceremony, although this is a very meaningful and significant part of the ritual on the Day of Atonement. It is described in Leviticus 16:20–28.

____ Chapter 8 ____

Exhortation #3: Move On to Maturity
Hebrews 5:11–6:12

The writer of Hebrews is really getting on a roll. He is excited to progress to the really juicy stuff, the deep things about the greatness of Jesus. But he has a problem. Many of his hearers are not ready to get to the deep things of God. We need the third of our five admonitions. This is an admonition that will not only prepare us to hear deep things, it will, if we accept it, help to ensure our salvation, so that what we hope for may be fully realized (Hebrews 6:11). What is it that we must do to be assured of our salvation?

We have much to say about this, but it is hard to make it clear to you because you no longer try to understand. In fact, though by this time you ought to be teachers, you need someone to teach you the elementary truths of God's word all over again. You need milk, not solid food! (Hebrews 5:11–12)

In other words, we need to GROW UP! Ouch! When our parents or a teacher told us to grow up, we did not take it as a compliment. It was not meant as one. Who of us wants to hear such an admonition? Many of us can remember our parents admonishing us, "Stop acting like a baby." To hear this means that we are still acting like spiritual children. God wants us to be child-like, but not to be childish. Although we have been Christians for many years, some of us have stopped growing. We remember the past when we grew rapidly, but such is no longer the case in our lives. Some of us have even regressed to the point that we are behind where we were several years ago in important aspects of our Christian walk. What a sorry state for a disciple of Jesus to be in.

The Greek word for "slow to learn" here is *nothros*. It means slow moving in mind, torpid, witlessly forgetful, dull of hearing. God has spoken to you through the Scriptures, through sermons and through your spiritual advisers, and you just are not getting it! Yours is a case of arrested development. You deliberately choose not to seek deeper understanding. You are a spiritual passive-aggressive. You are like the doctor who completed med school fifty years ago and does not bother to keep up with the latest medical advances. Would you want to go to such a doctor?

You know what they say; if you are not growing, you are going backward. And guess what, it is true! It has been said, "Whoever ceases to grow ceases to be good." Does this apply to you? In what ways are you more complete as a disciple of Jesus today than you were six months or two years ago? Can you list the areas of growth? Can you plot out the ways that the Holy Spirit has caused you to become more like Christ? If you struggle to call to mind areas of recent growth, then you had better listen to this exhortation.

If an infant has a diaper problem, we do not worry, but if a twenty-year-old does, we will be really concerned. If a six-month-old cannot speak, it is not a big deal, but if a preteen has trouble talking, we will definitely send him or her to a speech therapist. What is your personal expectation for Christian growth? Are there signs that you need a spiritual therapist? Have you become complacent? Is it time, right now, today, for you to get back to growing again? The writer of Hebrews suggests two essential areas of growth for us to consider. Let us take the opportunity to see how we measure up in these areas. The matters we will think about are knowledge in God's word and our own personal righteousness. Growth in the first ought to lead to growth in the second, but we can become stuck in either one.

> *Anyone who lives on milk, being still an infant, is not acquainted with the teaching about righteousness. But solid food is for the mature, who by constant use have trained themselves to distinguish good from evil.*
>
> *Therefore let us move beyond the elementary teachings about Christ and be taken forward to maturity, not laying again the foundation of repentance from acts that lead to death, and of faith in God, instruction about cleansing rites, the laying on of hands, the resurrection of the dead, and eternal judgment. And God permitting, we will do so.* (Hebrews 5:13–6:3)

Ask yourself right now: *How am I growing in my knowledge of God's word?* If you have been a Christian for ten, twenty or thirty years, you ought to have a truly profound grasp of the Scriptures. By now, hopefully, you have had perhaps five or ten thousand quiet times. What have you been learning? Do you have a plan? Or are you just playing it by ear and studying out the latest lesson you heard on Sunday? What book in the Bible have you studied recently to the point of knowing it truly in depth, so that you could expound its outline, theme, major points, connections with other passages and the meaning of important words, so that you could teach an in-depth class without notes, at a moment's notice? Which of the great Christian doctrines or which of God's qualities have you studied with such biblical depth that you can say with great confidence that you "get it?" And we are not talking about what you learned eight years ago. What are you learning now? What about the book of Hosea? Could you state the subject, and could you say from memory what is a theme passage for this book? If you have been a Christian fifteen years, surely you can.

As when we were spiritual infants, we need to "crave pure spiritual milk," so that by it we may grow up in our salvation (1 Peter 2:2). Some of us have been living on spiritual junk food. We settle for a few biblical nuggets and always go back to the same scriptures we have used for years. God wants to speak to us of "wisdom among the mature" but we are more attracted to "the wisdom of this age or of the rulers of this age" (1 Corinthians 2:6). God's goal for us is that "we all reach unity in the faith and in the knowledge of the Son of God and become mature, attaining to the whole measure of the fullness of Christ" (Ephesians 4:13). Is this your earnest, deep-seated desire?

Our intent here is not to make anyone feel guilty. This is not what the Hebrew writer is trying to do either. Later, in chapter 6, we will see that his goal in giving this admonition is that we be encouraged and confident in our salvation, not discouraged. He is trying to help ensure that we make it to heaven. For myself (John), I set a goal about twelve years ago to know every book in the Bible in depth. This is my long-term goal for now. I am just over half-way there. To achieve this, I have a short-term goal for this week and a medium-term goal for the next six months. In the process of following this plan, I can assure you that I have grown in my knowledge of the Bible as much in the last three years as in any previous three years of my Christian walk. This is as it should be. The greatest command includes that we love God with all of our minds. Let us do so.

The other area of expected growth in Hebrews 5 and 6 is in personal righteousness. God expects that we grow in knowledge, but he also expects us to grow in how we put this knowledge into practice. We need a healthy balance of the two. If we grow only in our knowledge of Scripture but not in our practice of personal righteousness, we become unbalanced. It is difficult to walk with one leg much longer than the other. If we want to be secure in our salvation (and who does not want that?), then through "constant use" we should "have trained [ourselves] to distinguish good from evil." And we are not talking about the basics here. The writer expects that we have put those "acts that lead to death" behind us a long time ago. It's great that you quit smoking before you were baptized, but you no longer get much credit for growth in that area. At this point in your life, not using profanity in your daily conversation anymore does not count as moving on to maturity.

Some of us have been worn down by the world. Rather than becoming more sensitive to sin, we are hardened to it. The movies that bothered us ten years ago hardly even bother us today. As stated in Hebrews 3:13, we have become "hardened by sin's deceitfulness." This is not good. Growth in righteousness ought to be the natural result of the Holy Spirit living in us, but it does not come about by accident. We need to *practice* righteousness. We need to struggle with all our might to acquire godly habits. We need to learn to distinguish good from evil in ever-more-subtle ways. We should be softer with regard to sin, not harder.

Notice that the writer tells us that we gain in our personal righteousness through "constant use." Muscles that get constant use grow. Through constant use of our bodies to, for example, drive a car or shoot a basketball, we gain muscle memory. If we have disciplined ourselves time and time again, then when we see someone dressed provocatively, when a situation arises in which it would be easy to deceive or when one of our emotional buttons is pushed, we are at the point that it now takes relatively little mental effort to steer clear of the temptation. We are a well-oiled, sin-avoiding person. Thank you, God, that we have the Holy Spirit who convicts us when we sin, if we are willing to walk by the Spirit. If you have significant weak points in your personal righteousness, then you will be held back from maturing. This could be the weakness that allows Satan to get a foothold. God is admonishing us to give attention to these weak points—to shore up our righteousness so that we can move on to the greater things that he has in mind for us. It is definitely worth the effort.

The next word in the text is "therefore." Generally, when the word "therefore" is used, there is a preceding assumption. In this case the writer is not assuming that you are fully mature, but he is assuming that you are fully on board and willing to put in the effort to grow in your knowledge of God and in your personal holiness. If this is so, excellent, then "let us move beyond the elementary teachings about Christ and be taken forward to maturity" (6:1).

But what if you are not willing to strive for maturity, or what if you have been stuck in a path of shrinking faith and righteousness for an extended period of time? In that case, perhaps you had better give attention to these basics. You are not ready to read the rest of Hebrews (but it is okay if you do anyway). You need to lay again "the foundation of repentance from acts that lead to death, and of faith in God, instruction about cleansing rites, the laying on of hands, the resurrection of the dead, and eternal judgment" (6:1b–2). The Greek word for foundation here is *stoicheia*, which roughly translates as the ABCs of biblical faith. We need to be rock solid in our convictions about the basics, which are repentance, faith, baptism (literally, washings), the indwelling of the Holy Spirit (more on this below), the resurrection of Christ and the reality of eternal judgment. Wavering on any of these basics makes us unprepared to move on to maturity.

For many of us, perhaps one of the ABCs listed may seem out of place. "The laying on of hands" is itemized as one of the *stoicheia* of the faith. For most of us, the laying on of hands is not part of the introductory Bible lessons we were taught before we were baptized. It is possible that the laying on of hands is a reference to the practice of appointing someone to a task (Acts 6:3–6, 13:3; 1 Timothy 4:14) or imparting a gift (Acts 8:17, 19:6; 2 Timothy 1:6). More likely it is a reference to the doctrine of the Holy Spirit. As early as the second half of the first century, the Church developed the tradition that one who was baptized, and who therefore received the Holy Spirit (Acts 2:38), would have hands laid on them as a symbol of having received the Spirit. This is not a biblical practice, of course. Eventually the Church developed the false teaching that the Holy Spirit was not given at baptism but was given later when the bishop who performed the baptism anointed the newly baptized with oil and laid hands on them. In any case, "the laying on of hands" in this passage is probably a reference to the doctrine of the indwelling of the Holy Spirit.

Again, our preacher is prepared to assume that most of his hearers are ready to move on to deeper things: "And God permitting, we will do so." But if this is not the case—if we have been thickheaded spiritually—then he has one of the sternest warnings in the entire Bible for us. God's intent is to encourage us, but for some of us, love requires the severest possible warning, not an encouragement. Others are doing well spiritually but are tempted to forget how serious it can be for those who are in spiritual decline.

> *It is impossible for those who have once been enlightened, who have tasted the heavenly gift, who have shared in the Holy Spirit, who have tasted the goodness of the word of God and the powers of the coming age and who have fallen away, to be brought back to repentance. To their loss they are crucifying the Son of God all over again and subjecting him to public disgrace.* (Hebrews 6:4–6)

This passage is not hard to interpret. We do not need a biblical scholar to understand what the word "impossible" means. It means that it cannot happen, no way, not ever. If we fall away, *as defined by the writer of Hebrews in this passage*, then it is all over for us. We cannot ever come back to repentance. It cannot possibly get more serious than this. We had better pay strict attention to this warning!

By the way, there are four things that are described as impossible in Hebrews. It is impossible:

1. **For those who have fallen away to be renewed to repentance (6:4)**
2. **For God to lie (6:18)**
3. **For the blood of bulls and goats to remove sins (10:4)**
4. **To please God without faith (11:6)**

We have already mentioned that the majority of those who are of the evangelical faith are taught the "once saved, always saved" doctrine that is the product of Calvinist theology. What do they do with this passage? As we described earlier, Calvinists want to apply this warning, not to saved people, but to a mythical group of Jewish people who have been attending church for a long time but have not yet become Christians. This idea is completely ruled out by the description in this passage of the one who falls away. This person has "been enlightened." Scholars of church history[6] tell us that "enlightened" was used in the primitive Church as a kind of shorthand for one who has been baptized. This person has tasted the gift, presumably of salvation, has received the indwelling Holy Spirit and has tasted the powers of the coming age, presumably as a part of the kingdom of God. It is ludicrous to propose that this is not a reference to a Christian. This warning is for us who have been saved. Yes, we can fall away, and if we do, then for us there is no coming back. It will be too late for us. Peter said about the same set of persons, "Of them the proverbs are true: 'A dog returns to its vomit' and 'A sow that is washed returns to her wallowing in the mud.'" (2 Peter 2:22). If we fall away we are worse off than we were before when we were lost, because at least then we had hope. We could repent and be saved.

Perhaps this is not what you have been taught. Perhaps you have been in the habit of describing as fallen away one who is deeply struggling with sin or who is doing so poorly spiritually as to not even attend a true biblical Christian church. We should be extremely cautious about using this term! To say definitively that a person has fallen away in the sense described in Hebrews 6 means that there is no way that they can ever be restored to faith—period. It seems that only God has a right to make such a strong judgment. Perhaps you are feeling even now some frustration that you were taught to use the term "fallen away" incorrectly.

We want to be careful what we say here. The fact is that in the Bible, the phrase "fallen away" is used in more than one sense. In Matthew 11:6 and Luke 7:23 we find the expression "those who have fallen away on account of me" in some translations, whereas others talk about stumbling because of Jesus or being offended by him. It is not wrong or improper to refer to someone who has drifted from Christ as fallen away (given that Jesus did this), but it can be confusing in light of Hebrews 6:4–6. Let us make a suggestion. If you know of someone who has become a Christian but who is not currently active in their faith, who may very well be on the way toward losing salvation, perhaps you could refer to this person as not currently faithful, as a prodigal, or as not a member of the church and leave the matter of whether this person has permanently lost their salvation in the hands of God.

It is our intention to study Hebrews chapter by chapter. However, the issue of falling away is so central to the teaching of Hebrews that we want to give a more complete description of the doctrine of falling away in the context of Hebrews 6:4–6. This passage certainly gets our attention with its dramatic warning, but it does leave some aspects of this doctrine unclear. For this reason, let us move forward to the other major passage in Hebrews that discusses the extremely serious possibility of falling away. It is Hebrews 10:26–31. This is the most profound warning in all of the New Testament.

If we deliberately keep on sinning after we have received the knowledge of the truth, no sacrifice for sins is left, but only a fearful expectation of judgment and of raging fire that will consume the enemies of God. Anyone who rejected the law of Moses died without mercy on the testimony of two or three witnesses. How much more severely do you think someone deserves to be punished who has trampled the Son of God underfoot, who has treated as an unholy thing the blood of the covenant that sanctified them, and who has insulted the Spirit of grace? For we know him who said, "It is mine to avenge; I will repay," and again, "The Lord will judge his people." It is a dreadful thing to fall into the hands of the living God.

Here we see more specifically what could cause us to lose our salvation, as well as what the results of falling away from grace are. Let us look carefully at this most sobering passage. What will result in us losing our salvation? It is continual, willful, deliberate sin. Thus, there are two qualities to the sin that will lead to apostasy: *continual* and *deliberate*.

The Greek word for deliberate here is *hekousios*, which means willingly, deliberately, intentionally. It has already been noted that there was no means of forgiveness for deliberate sin in the Old Testament, at least not in the sacrificial system. The sacrifices were designed to make atonement for sins committed without intent.

The LORD said to Moses, "Say to the Israelites: 'When anyone sins unintentionally and does what is forbidden in any of the LORD's commands.... If the whole Israelite community sins unintentionally and does what is forbidden in any of the LORD's commands, even though the community is unaware of the matter, when they realize their guilt and the sin they committed becomes known, the assembly must bring a young bull as a sin offering....'" The LORD said to Moses: "When anyone is unfaithful to the LORD by sinning unintentionally in regard to any of the LORD's holy things, they are to bring to the LORD as a penalty a ram from the flock." (Leviticus 4:1–2, 4:13–14, 5:14–15, emphasis added)

There was no provision in the law for forgiveness of intentional murder, blasphemy against God, adultery, idolatry and other sins that could not be committed accidentally.

What is deliberate sin?

> But anyone who sins defiantly, whether native-born or foreigner, blasphemes the LORD and must be cut off from the people of Israel. Because they have despised the LORD's word and broken his commands, they must surely be cut off; their guilt remains on them. (Numbers 15:30–31)

To illustrate deliberate sin, consider a child who pushes its food off the high chair onto the floor. The parent tells the child not to do this. The child does it again. The parent looks the child in the eyes and tells it, "Do not push your food dish onto the floor." The child looks the parent straight in the eyes and pushes the dish onto the floor anyway. This is an illustration of what we are talking about. Signing a false tax return, typing into our computer the address of a pornographic website, walking out of a restaurant without paying the bill: these are deliberate sins. Most likely all of us have committed deliberate sins, even after baptism, but for the majority of us this is a rare occurrence. We are not in the habit of willfully rebelling against God. But we commit unintentional sins every day. For these acts, we have a high priest who is able to empathize with our weakness, and we can approach the throne of grace with confidence to receive mercy in our time of need (Hebrews 4:15–16). We should be very thankful for the grace and mercy of our faithful high priest Jesus. And we should feel confident about our forgiveness as well. This is what God wants for us.

But willful sin is in another category. We need to take this kind of sin very seriously. God does not tolerate open rebellion. However, even with this kind of sin, it is only if we "keep on sinning" in this way that we are in danger of losing our salvation. Fortunately, we are under the new covenant (Hebrews 8:8–13), and even deliberate sin that is not continual is forgiven by the blood of Jesus. We can be assured that God is immeasurably patient with us. He is more patient with us, even in deliberate sin, than we would be if we were judging ourselves. It is difficult to fall away once we have been forgiven and received the Holy Spirit. "The Lord is gracious and compassionate, slow to anger and rich in love" (Psalm 145:8).

Nevertheless, we are solemnly cautioned here, and it would be irresponsible and foolish to ignore the warning of Hebrews 10:26–31.

If we deliberately and continually sin, what may be the eventual result of such blatant defiance of God? "No sacrifice for sins is left, but only a fearful expectation of judgment and of raging fire that will consume the enemies of God." We could come again into judgment for our sins and go to hell. Here the Hebrew writer uses an illustration from the law of Moses. Most likely, he is referring to Deuteronomy 17:2–7. If anyone was guilty of the willful sin of idolatry, and if there were multiple witnesses to this act, then the guilty party was to be stoned to death by the people. This is intense stuff, folks. God is trying to get our attention here. He asks us, "How much more severely do you think someone deserves to be punished who has trampled the Son of God underfoot, who has treated as an unholy thing the blood of the covenant that sanctified them, and who has insulted the Spirit of grace?" The answer to this rhetorical question is this: immeasurably more severely! Surely eternity in hell is more severe than being stoned to death.

In case there was any doubt that we are talking about a Christian here, the Hebrew writer is describing a person who has already been sanctified. The one who willfully and continually sins after receiving sanctification is insulting the Holy Spirit and spitting on the blood of Jesus. He or she is committing sacrilege—treating as a common thing that which is holy. "Jesus died for me? Whatever..." God WILL NOT tolerate this behavior. Continual and willful sin is not merely breaking some law; it is destroying our personal relationship with God and deeply wounding his heart. At some point the Holy Spirit will leave us, and when he does, we are left defenseless. Jesus is no longer our advocate. We come back into judgment, and as we already said, our condition is worse than it was before our salvation because "it is impossible...to be brought back to repentance" (6:4–6). This is "the sin that leads to death" of 1 John 5:16. It is not any particular single sin; rather, it is willful and continual rebellion, after we have been saved. This is the blaspheming of the Holy Spirit spoken of in Matthew 12:31–32, Mark 3:28–30 and Luke 12:10. If we deliberately and continually set out to sin against the one who saved us, then we are blaspheming the Holy Spirit who lives in us, and we are warned most solemnly, "It is mine to avenge; I will repay" (quoting Deuteronomy 32:35–36) and "It is a dreadful thing to fall into the hands of the living God."

To summarize, what is the unforgivable sin? It is:

- **Crucifying the Son of God all over again (Hebrews 6:6)**

- Subjecting Jesus to public disgrace (Hebrews 6:6)
- Trampling the Son of God under foot (Hebrews 10:29)
- Showing disdain for the blood of Jesus (Hebrews 10:29)
- Insulting the Holy Spirit (Hebrews 10:29)
- Blaspheming the Holy Spirit (Matthew 12:32)

Let us return to Hebrews 6;

> *For ground that has drunk the rain that has often fallen on it and that produces vegetation useful to those it is cultivated for, receives a blessing from God. But if it produces thorns and thistles, it is worthless and about to be cursed, and will be burned at the end.* (Hebrews 6:7-8)

If we "ignore so great a salvation" (Hebrews 2:3), and if we deliberately and continually sin, then the result will be that the "ground" which is our lives will produce only thorns and thistles. We make ourselves worthless to God. Thorns and thistles are inedible and are therefore not useful to grazing lambs and cattle. In the same way, our lives will not be useful to the master if we return to the pigpen of sin.

This is what was taught by Jesus in the parable of the talents. (Matthew 25:14-30) This parable falls between the parable of the ten virgins and that of the sheep and goats. In the context, it is about who will be with God for eternity. At the end of the story about the servants and their stewardship of the talents given them, the one who did not produce a crop was told, "So take the talent from him and give it to the one who has 10 talents. For to everyone who has, more will be given and he will have more than enough. But from the one who does not have, even what he has will be taken away from him. And throw this good-for-nothing slave into outer darkenss. In that place there will be weeping and gnalshing of teeth." (Matthew 25:28-30 HCSB) Is your life producing fruit useful to God, or is it producing mostly thistles and thorns? All of us want to be useful to God, but it is not just a matter of what we want, God requires that his investment in us produces a return.

Perhaps those of us with a sensitive conscience are feeling overwhelmed right now, and perhaps some of us ought to feel this way to some extent. But we need to remember that the purpose of the Hebrew writer is to get us back on the right footing, and his intent is far more to give us assurance of our salvation than it is to strike fear into our hearts. In Hebrews 6:9-12, we are reminded that it is the purpose of God in the book of Hebrews to encourage us, not to condemn us. We need a glass of fresh, cool water, and God gives it to us.

> *Even though we speak like this, dear friends, we are convinced of better things in your case—the things that have to do with salvation. God is not unjust; he will not forget your work and the love you have shown him as you have helped his people and continue to help them. We want each of you to show this same diligence to the very end, so that what you hope for may be fully realized. We do not want you to become lazy, but to imitate those who through faith and patience inherit what has been promised. (Hebrews 6:9–12)*

God is not some sort of evil taskmaster; quite the opposite. It is his desire that we experience a blessed life now and that we obtain a rich reward in the future. We are in a marathon and have not yet reached the end of the race, but the work we did in the first few miles is already producing for us a reward, which we will receive when we cross the finish line. This should give us great encouragement to make it to the end.

I (John) climbed Mount Whitney just a couple of days before writing these words. This is the highest peak in the lower forty-eight states of the USA. When I reached the ninth of eleven miles and 13,400 out of 14,500 feet of elevation, I was utterly exhausted. But there was just something about the fact that the peak lay within my sight that kept me going. There was no way I was going to give up and turn back. The reward we have at the peak of our own mountain is immeasurably greater than the satisfaction of topping a challenging physical mountain. God is not asking something unreasonable of us. He is simply asking us to continue in our diligence until the end. Oh, it is worth it. Can you imagine the foolishness of giving up our race when we have come this far? The writer of Hebrews, and therefore God, is walking along the path toward heaven right beside us. You can do it. I am very confident in you. God, your Father is as well, and Jesus is advocating for you at his right hand. Consider the great reward.

Have you been tempted to become lazy in your walk? Well, guess what, you are not alone. But the solution is really quite simple. <u>Consider the reward ahead of you, remember the reason you began to follow Jesus in the first place and get back into the race</u>. Let us face the persecution that is coming soon (the situation for the audience of Hebrews), or let us face the current drought in our walk with Jesus, the turbulence in the local church or the temptation that has recently come back to haunt us, and let us simply look to Jesus, the one who is the reason we got into this in the beginning. You can do it, and you will do it.

If you do not have it in yourself to get back up on your horse and continue your ride with diligence, then the writer of Hebrews asks you to consider those who have already completed the race. You know people who have already made it, and you know that they endured at least as much as you have, yet they remained faithful to the end. You went to their memorial service and you were deeply inspired by their example. Can you take your eyes off your own situation long enough to "consider the outcome of their way of life and imitate their faith"? (Hebrews 13:7). Yes, you can. As our Spanish-speaking friends would tell us, "Sí, se puede!"

End Notes _____

7. Scholars divide the psalms into several categories. One of these is the royal psalms, which are poems dedicated to the kingly aspect of God or the prophetic nature of the kingship of David and its relationship to Jehovah as king of the Jews. The royal psalms include Psalm 110, of course, as well as Psalms 2, 18, 20, 21, 45, 72, 101, 132 and 144.

Chapter 9

Jesus Is Greater Than Abraham: Great Assurance of Salvation
Hebrews 6:13–20a

In this little section of Hebrews we see that Jesus is superior to Abraham. We are also given the greatest assurance of our salvation found in the book of Hebrews. We are told that if we stay faithful we certainly will be saved in the end.

> When God made his promise to Abraham, since there was no one greater for him to swear by, he swore by himself, saying, "I will surely bless you and give you many descendants." And so after waiting patiently, Abraham received what was promised.
>
> People swear by someone greater than themselves, and the oath confirms what is said and puts an end to all argument. Because God wanted to make the unchanging nature of his purpose very clear to the heirs of what was promised, he confirmed it with an oath. God did this so that, by two unchangeable things in which it is impossible for God to lie, we who have fled to take hold of the hope set before us may be greatly encouraged. We have this hope as an anchor for the soul, firm and secure. It enters the inner sanctuary behind the curtain, where our forerunner, Jesus, has entered on our behalf. (Hebrews 6:13–20a)

God wants us to live in extreme confidence of our salvation and he wants us to know absolutely that we have an advocate with him in heaven. This confidence will serve us well when we go through times of spiritual challenge such as what the recipients of Hebrews are about to go through. These trials may require patience, as Abraham waited patiently. (v. 15) One interesting point about this passage is that it is not immediately clear what promise he wants us to be so sure about. Perhaps he wants us to, like Abraham, trust all of his promises to us. More likely, the specific promise he has in mind is that found in Hebrews 4:1, which is that if we remain faithful to the end we will surely enter his rest—heaven. In the context of the passage, the promise involves "the hope set before us," which is the hope of heaven, making it likely that the writer has the promise in Hebrews 4:1 in mind.

How confident does God want us to be that we will make it to our own promised land? He wants us to be so assured of our salvation that he is willing to swear an oath on it. Our culture has mostly lost the tradition of swearing in the name of someone or something in order to put the stamp on a promise we have made. It was only a generation or two ago that it was common to hear people saying things like "I swear to God" or "I swear by the Bible." We have a remnant of such oaths used in our court systems, in which people swear to tell the truth "so help me God." Although we are not much used to this practice of swearing oaths, we can easily get the concept. When someone makes a promise and wants to make the one to whom they are promising confident that the promise will be completed, they swear by someone or something greater than themselves. The Jews were in the habit of swearing by the temple, by the mercy seat in the temple or by heaven.

Nevertheless, it is odd that God would swear by anything at all, is it not? In at least one case in the New Testament, we are told not to make any oaths (Matthew 5:34–37). It is a bit awkward for God to swear to something he has promised us. Surely, those who believe in God believe him when he makes a promise. Yet there are very rare times when the one to whom the promise is made really needs assurance. Such was the case when God asked Abraham to kill his one and only legitimate son and heir (such may be our case after reading Hebrews 6:4-8). Abraham's faith was so great that he was willing to sacrifice the son whom God had earlier promised him. In Genesis 22:16–18 God tells Abraham:

> *"I swear by myself, declares the LORD, that because you have done this and have not withheld your son, your only son, I will surely bless you and make your descendants as numerous as the stars in the sky and as the sand on the seashore. Your descendants will take possession of the cities of their enemies, and through your offspring all nations on earth will be blessed."*

God has fulfilled every single one of the promises he made to Abraham. This can gives us great confidence that he will fulfill his promise to us found in Hebrews that we will be with him forever.

The Hebrew writer uses a human argument here. If people swear by something greater than themselves in order that we can trust their promises, surely we can trust God if he swears an oath. But who is greater than God? No one, of course, so God swears by himself. The Hebrew writer tells us that God swears by two unchangeable things: 1) his word (i.e., the promise or the oath) and 2) himself. And just in case you were not confident that God will do what he says, we are reminded that it is literally impossible for God to lie (Numbers 23:19; 1 Samuel 15:29). Hopefully we are getting the message here. God wants us to live, not in fear, but in highly confident expectation that we will make it to heaven. Not only that, he wants us to live in faith and hope because we have a great high priest in heaven advocating for us before the throne of God. The word "promise" appears fifteen times in Hebrews, which is more than in any other book in the Bible. Again, God wants us to live confidently.

One thing to note about the book of Hebrews is that the two most solemn warnings, Hebrews 6:4–8 and Hebrews 10:26–31, are joined by the two most emphatic assurances of our eternal salvation, Hebrews 6:13–19 and Hebrews 10:19–22. God wants us to be made fully aware of the danger of apostasy, but he does not want to overwhelm us with this truth. He wants us, in the end, to be confident that our relationship with him, both in this life and in eternity, is secured if we will hold on to his promises as did Abraham.

There are two closely connected words used repeatedly in this section. They are "promise" and "hope." The biblical use of the word "hope" is very different from the standard English meaning. In common usage, when we say we hope something will happen, we mean that it is highly likely it will *not* happen. "I hope I get an A." Biblical hope is of a quite different nature. The hope God holds out for us in Hebrews is more like confident expectation. One of the most encouraging verses in all of Scripture is found right here. It is Hebrews 6:19: "We have this hope as an anchor for the soul, firm and secure. It enters the inner sanctuary behind the curtain." This hope we have, of course, is Jesus Christ. In the ancient world, the anchor was a symbol of hope. Commentators debate whether the anchor metaphor applies to the hope we have, to the promise made on oath, or to Jesus himself. The answer is simply, yes—it is all three. In the primitive Church, one of the most common symbols used to represent Christ was the anchor, because of this very passage of Scripture (it is the only one in the New Testament that uses the anchor as a metaphor).

What is an anchor used for? It is used to prevent something that is movable from moving. Spend some time right now contemplating the fact that we have Jesus as an anchor for our souls. We have a hope that will not move or change. Nothing can move us because nothing can move Jesus from his place in the heavenly tabernacle with the Father. He is the true high priest. He is in the inner sanctuary—not the one that is merely a copy, but the real one, the one in heaven, as we will see later in Hebrews.

This brings us to Hebrews 6:20, which is the transitional verse to our next section. Christ is the anchor for our souls behind the curtain, "where our forerunner, Jesus, has entered on our behalf." The word "forerunner" in Greek is *prodromos*. Literally, it means the one who runs ahead of the others. Metaphorically, it is the pioneer, the one who leads the way, the one who checks out the lay of the land to make sure that it is safe for others to enter and settle there. Daniel Boone was the pioneer who opened up Kentucky and Tennessee to settlement by Europeans. Jesus is the pioneer who opens the heavenly realms for us to occupy them. He has declared them safe and ready for occupation.

To the Jews, the most holy place, the holy of holies, the inner sanctuary, was the place where God dwelt. It was where the *shekinah*—the glory of God—was seated. When Solomon's temple was consecrated, the Lord entered the holy of holies. "When the priests withdrew from the Holy Place, the cloud filled the temple of the Lord. And the priests could not perform their service because of the cloud, for the glory of the Lord filled the temple" (1 Kings 8:10). From this time forward, no Jew could enter the most holy place on pain of immediate death. As we have said before, only the high priest had this privilege, and only on one day of the year, for only a few moments. But Jesus is the pioneer who shows us the way to enter the very presence of God. Why? Because he is a priest in the order of Melchizedek.

____ Chapter 10 ____

Jesus' Priesthood Is
Greater Than Aaron's
Hebrews 6:20b–7:28

We are now ready to embark upon the heart of the book of Hebrews. The first six chapters were, in a sense, setting us up for what we will learn in chapter 7, in which we find the core of the argument in this amazing sermon. As a priest in the order of Melchizedek, Jesus is our great, unique and awesome high priest—the one who gives us access to the Father.

This is deep teaching. The fact that it will be tough going to understand Hebrews 7 was set up by the writer in 5:11 when we were told, "We have much to say about this [the priesthood of Jesus], but it is hard to make it clear to you." What is the order of Melchizedek, and what does it have to do with our relationship with God as followers of Jesus? Let us get started.

He has become a high priest forever, in the order of Melchizedek.

This Melchizedek was king of Salem and priest of God Most High. He met Abraham returning from the defeat of the kings and blessed him, and Abraham gave him a tenth of everything. First, the name Melchizedek means "king of righteousness"; then also, "king of Salem" means "king of peace." Without father or mother, without genealogy, without beginning of days or end of life, resembling the Son of God, he remains a priest forever.

Just think how great he was: Even the patriarch Abraham gave him a tenth of the plunder! Now the law requires the descendants of Levi who become priests to collect a tenth from the people—that is, from their fellow Israelites—even though they also are descended from Abraham. This man, however, did not trace his descent from Levi, yet he collected a tenth from Abraham and blessed him who had the promises. And without doubt the lesser is blessed by the greater. In the

one case, the tenth is collected by people who die; but in the
other case, by him who is declared to be living. One might
even say that Levi, who collects the tenth, paid the tenth
through Abraham, because when Melchizedek met Abraham,
Levi was still in the body of his ancestor. (Hebrews 6:20b–7:10)

The writer of Hebrews is trying to do two things simultaneously here. He is trying to establish that the priesthood of Melchizedek, and therefore the high priesthood of Jesus, is superior to that of Levi. In addition, he is trying to establish the type/antitype relationship between Melchizedek and Jesus in order that we can truly understand what a great high priest we have. The former argument to explain the relationship between Levi and Melchizedek is perhaps a bit obscure to us, but the latter argument showing the parallels between Jesus and Melchizedek will be crystal clear when we look at all the evidence.

Before we dive into the argument in Hebrews 7, let us first consider what we know about this enigmatic figure Melchizedek from the Old Testament. The fact is that we do not know a lot about him, but we will find that every single thing we do know will turn out to be of great symbolic importance. In the Bible God can say a lot with very few words. The only two passages that mention Melchizedek are Genesis 14:18–20 and Psalm 110:4. That is only four verses!

Then Melchizedek king of Salem brought out bread and
wine. He was priest of God Most High, and he blessed Abram,
saying,

"Blessed be Abram by God Most High,
　　Creator of heaven and earth.
And praise be to God Most High,
　　who delivered your enemies unto your hand."
Then Abraham gave him a tenth of everything.
(Genesis 14:18–20)

The bare facts are these: After winning a battle against Kedorlaomer the Elamite, Abraham brought the spoils of the battle to Melchizedek, who was a priest of Yahweh and also the king of the city of Salem. Apparently Melchizedek was not related by birth to Abraham. Therefore, he was not "Jewish." When Abraham brought the spoils of the battle gained by the help of the Most High God, Melchizedek pronounced a blessing on Abraham in the name of God, and Abraham offered a tithe of the spoils of war to Melchizedek.

From this point we hear nothing whatsoever about Melchizedek in Scripture for more than eight hundred years. What did the Jews think about Melchizedek? Finally, after more than eight centuries of biblical silence, we have what would be one of the most puzzling passages in the entire Old Testament in a royal psalm of David.[7] Puzzling, that is, until the meaning is revealed in Hebrews: "The Lord has sworn and will not change his mind: 'You are a priest forever, in the order of Melchizedek.'"

The writer of Hebrews makes this a prophecy of the Messiah. Is he taking this passage out of context? Would this be understood as a messianic prophecy, even to a Jewish person who did not know about Jesus? The answer is yes. This is a royal psalm, written by David. Surely David did not see himself as a priest, never mind as a priest forever. Consider again Psalm 110:1:

> The LORD says to my lord:
>   "Sit at my right hand
> until I make your enemies
>   a footstool for your feet."

The lord to whom the Lord is speaking is the Messiah. He is the branch of Jesse (Isaiah 11:1). There is no possible way that David is talking about himself. He is speaking of the one he is a prefigure of as king of Israel, which is the Messiah, Jesus, the descendant of David. Therefore, with Psalm 110 we are left for more than one thousand years with this prophecy: The Messiah who is coming will be a priest, but not a priest from Levi. Rather, he will be a priest in the order of Melchizedek. Thankfully, Hebrews completes this picture. Otherwise, we would be left quite confused.

Now, using these two passages as the background, let us proceed to what we learn about the priesthood of Jesus in Hebrews. Remember that there are two arguments here—one comparing Melchizedek to Levi and one drawing parallels between Jesus and Melchizedek. First, let us consider what God tells us in Hebrews about the priesthood, not of Jesus, but of Melchizedek. After the battle with Kedorlaomer, Abraham brought the spoils of the battle to Melchizedek. The Hebrew writer reminds us in Hebrews 7:1–2 and 4 of the two things that happened: Melchizedek blessed Abraham, and Abraham gave a tithe of the plunder to Melchizedek.

This is how the writer of Hebrews interprets these facts as they relate to Melchizedek: "Just think how great he was: Even the patriarch Abraham gave him a tenth of the plunder!" Here is where the argument gets a bit difficult to follow. "This man, however, did not trace his descent from Levi, yet he collected a tenth from Abraham and blessed him who had the promises. And without doubt the lesser is blessed by the greater." In other words, Melchizedek is "greater" than Abraham. By implication, Jesus is also greater than Abraham, which completes the argument that Jesus is greater than Abraham begun in Hebrews 6:13–20. This does not mean that Melchizedek is better than Abraham, any more than the Father is "better" than the Son or the husband is "better" than the wife. This is a positional authority.

The next argument is probably the most difficult to follow in all of Hebrews. In 7:9 we are told that "one might even say that Levi, who collects the tenth [i.e., the Levitical priests who collect tithes from Israel], paid the tenth through Abraham, because when Melchizedek met Abraham, Levi was still in the body of his ancestor." What we have just been given is biblical "proof" that the priesthood of Melchizedek is superior positionally to the priesthood of Aaron. Melchizedek is greater than Abraham; Levi is the descendant of Abraham; therefore the priesthood of Levi is inferior to that of Melchizedek. This argument may seem to us a bit of a stretch, but it is logical, and it comes straight from the mouth of God through the writer of Hebrews. To believers in Christ, that is good enough for us.

So, the priesthood of Melchizedek is greater than that of Levi. Next, we come to the second argument in Hebrews 7, which is that Jesus is a priest in the order of Melchizedek, and therefore his priesthood is greater than that of Levi. The two arguments are intertwined, so we will have to go back to earlier verses in Hebrews 7 to complete the case for the priesthood of Jesus. Here the argument turns to type/antitype examples regarding Melchizedek and Jesus. Melchizedek is a prefigure of Jesus.

There are a great many things about Melchizedek that parallel Jesus. Some of these are fairly obvious, but others are less apparent at first glance. "First, the name Melchizedek means 'king of righteousness'" (v. 2). Both Melchizedek and Jesus are kings, and both of them are righteous kings. Melchizedek was not without sin, but his name literally meant king of righteousness. Jesus, as the antitype, is a righteous king, not merely by having the name, but because he was the only person ever to live to adulthood who was without sin (John 8:46). Jesus fulfills the prophecy anticipated by Melchizedek's name.

Next there is the fact that the name of the city over which Melchizedek ruled as king also creates a type/antitype relationship. It is not a coincidence that Melchizedek just so happened to rule over the city of Salem (which was later renamed Jerusalem). The word *"Salem"* in Hebrew is shalom, which, as most of us know, means peace. Melchizedek was literally the king of peace. Who else in all of history has been known as the king of peace? That is not a hard question. Jesus is the King of peace. With both of the type/antitype relationships we have considered, Melchizedek is these two things by what could be considered a historical accident. He is king of righteousness by the accident of having the name, and he is the king of peace by another "accident," the name of his city. Jesus is these two things in reality. As with all type/antitype relationships between the Old and the New Testaments, the thing in the Old Testament is a shadow and "the reality, however, is found in Christ" (Colossians 2:17). This is great stuff. The Bible is clearly inspired by God. Could any schemer have pulled this off even if they tried? No! Truly, as Jesus said, "These are the very Scriptures that testify about me" (John 5:39).

Also, note that before Melchizedek was the king of peace he was the king of righteousness. He received his name before he became king of Salem. We must first have righteousness before we can have peace.

But when we are talking about Melchizedek as a prefigure of Messiah Jesus we are just getting started! The list of parallels continues: "Without father or mother, without genealogy, without beginning of days or end of life, resembling the Son of God, he remains a priest forever." We have already pointed out that Hebrews 7:9–10 is the most difficult argument in Hebrews. This one is a close second. The writer of Hebrews uses some of the many things we do not know about Melchizedek to extend the list of parallels between the two priests in the order of Melchizedek. We do not know the names of his parents, and we know nothing of his descendants. Therefore he has no (known) genealogy. In this, Melchizedek is like Jesus, as he had no human father, and he had no descendants because "he was cut off from the land of the living" (Isaiah 53:8). The argument the Hebrew writer uses here is not one any of us would probably be willing to make. He is arguing, not from any actual statement in the Bible,but from the silence of the Scriptures. Surely Melchizedek had actual parents, although we do not know their names. Whether he had descendants or not we simply do not know. But the Hebrew writer uses what we do not know about Melchizedek as an argument that he is a prefigure of Jesus.

Argument from the silence of Scripture was quite common to Jewish rabbinical interpretation of the Old Testament, even if it is surprising to us. The rabbis described four levels of meaning in a text:

1. **Peshat:** The literal, factual meaning of the text
2. **Remaz:** The suggested meaning of the text
3. **Derush:** The meaning arrived at after long and careful consideration of the text
4. **Sod:** The inner, allegorical or metaphorical meaning of the text

Experience tells us that we, as uninspired interpreters, should be wary of allegorizing the text of the Old Testament. We should avoid using the principle of *sod* in our hermeneutics. If we read Philo, the great Jewish teacher of the first century, we will discover that allegorizing often allows us to simply read our own philosophy into the Scriptures. However, with Hebrews we have inspired allegory. Its inspiration is established by the amazing result—the beauty of the conclusion the Hebrew writer reaches—and simply because Hebrews is part of the received canon of Scripture.

God is making a profound point about Jesus here. With the priesthood of Aaron, genealogy is everything (Ezra 2:3–63; Nehemiah 7:63–65). With the priesthood of Melchizedek, genealogy is not important—in fact, the lack of genealogy is a positive. Why? Because both Melchizedek and Jesus were chosen directly by God as priests, not because of descent, but because of their righteousness. Which is better, to have the right genealogy or the right life? We do not know Melchizedek's genealogy and we do not know about his descendants. However, what we know about Melchizedek is that, unlike priests in the order of Aaron, who are priests merely because of who their father was, Melchizedek was chosen as priest because of his own personal righteousness. This is another prophetic parallel between him and Jesus.

Then our author makes an additional argument. We know nothing of the death of Melchizedek; it is not recorded in the Scriptures (although we assume that he most likely did actually die eventually!). The writer of Hebrews makes a striking parallel here. We do not know when or even if Melchizedek died. Similarly, Jesus, although he died, was raised from the dead and still lives. Therefore, by parallel, both Melchizedek and Jesus remain "a priest forever." The argument that Melchizedek is a priest forever is made by the writer of Hebrews based on the fact that we know nothing of his death. Again, this argument from silence is not one we would be so bold as to make, but the inspired writer of Hebrews makes it, and we are sticking with it!

Qualities of Melchizedek's Priesthood
 A source of peace
 Based on personal righteousness
 Royal (king and priest simultaneously)
 Not inherited
 Eternal

We will find more messianic prefigure in Melchizedek in the next section:

> If perfection could have been attained through the Levitical priesthood—and indeed the law given to the people established that priesthood—why was there still need for another priest to come, one in the order of Melchizedek, not in the order of Aaron? For when the priesthood is changed, the law must be changed also. He of whom these things are said belonged to a different tribe, and no one from that tribe has ever served at the altar. For it is clear that our Lord descended from Judah, and in regard to that tribe Moses said nothing about priests. And what we have said is even more clear if another priest like Melchizedek appears, one who has become a priest not on the basis of a regulation as to his ancestry but on the basis of the power of an indestructible life. For it is declared:
>
> > "You are a priest forever,
> >   in the order of Melchizedek."
>
> The former regulation is set aside because it was weak and useless (for the law made nothing perfect), and a better hope is introduced, by which we draw near to God.
> And it was not without an oath! Others became priests without any oath, but he became a priest with an oath when God said to him:
>
> > "The Lord has sworn
> >   and will not change his mind:
> >   'You are a priest forever.'"
>
> Because of this oath, Jesus has become the guarantor of a better covenant.

Now there have been many of those priests, since death prevented them from continuing in office; but because Jesus lives forever, he has a permanent priesthood. Therefore he is able to save completely those who come to God through him, because he always lives to intercede for them. (Hebrews 7:11–25)

The next parallel that the writer of Hebrews makes between Melchizedek and Jesus is that neither is from the tribe of Levi. In the case of Jesus, he is from Judah, concerning which tribe Moses said nothing about priests. In the case of Melchizedek, he is also not from the tribe of Levi, since he is not even a Jew. Jesus is a priest because of the power that comes from his indestructible life (v. 16). There are a couple of other type/antitype parallels between Jesus and Melchizedek that deserve mention, even though the writer does not bring them out. First, Melchizedek was a priest primarily to Gentiles, not to Jews. Jesus is the high priest of both Jew and Gentile. Second, although it is not mentioned in Hebrews 7, we learn in Genesis 14:18 that when Abraham came to Melchizedek the offering he was given was bread and wine. Melchizedek offered bread and wine, and Jesus offers us his body and blood, as we remember by taking bread and wine in the Lord's Supper. A summary of the parallels between Melchizedek and Jesus is found in the table below.

Melchizedek	*Jesus*
Name means king of righteousness	Is a righteous king
King of a city with the name Peace	The King of peace
Without (known) genealogy	Has no genealogy
Without (known) end of days, therefore a priest forever	A priest forever
Physical king of physical Jerusalem	Spiritual king of spiritual Jerusalem
A greater priest than Levi	Greater than Abraham and therefore greater than Levi
A priest for Gentiles, not Jews	A priest for Gentiles and Jews
A priest due to character, not descent	A priest due to character, not descent
Gave Abraham bread and wine	Remembered by taking bread and wine

Having established that Jesus is of the priesthood of Melchizedek, which is superior to that of Aaron, and having established the unmistakable type/antitype relationship between the him and Melchizedek, we now return to the chief concern of the central section of Hebrews, which is the greatness of Jesus as a high priest. For the writer of Hebrews, the perfection of Jesus as high priest is the basis for the superiority of his covenant to the covenant of Moses (Hebrews 8), the superiority of the tabernacle where he ministers to the Jewish tabernacle/temple (Hebrews 9:1–10) and the superiority of the sacrifice of Jesus to the Mosaic sacrificial system (Hebrews 9:11–10:18). It is hard to overestimate the importance of Jesus as a great high priest to the entire book of Hebrews.

In verse 11 we are asked the rhetorical question, "If perfection could have been attained through the Levitical priesthood...why was there still need for another priest to come, one in the order of Melchizedek, not in the order of Aaron?" The answer, of course, is that perfection (*teleiosis:* perfection, wholeness, completeness) was not obtained through the old covenant or through the Levitical priesthood. We have already been told why the Levitical priesthood was imperfect—because the priests died, because they were not themselves righteous, because it was attained by accident of birth, because the Levites did not know the things of the Father as Jesus does and for many other reasons.

Next the writer of Hebrews makes the argument that if the priesthood is changed, then as a consequence law and the covenant must change as well: "For when the priesthood is changed, the law must be changed also" (v. 12). We might have made a different argument. We might have argued that the covenant establishes the priesthood, therefore a change in covenant will produce a change in priesthood. But in Hebrews it is the reverse. The Levitical priesthood was imperfect and needed to be replaced by a perfect eternal priesthood—the order of Melchizedek. Therefore, a new covenant must be produced to support that priesthood. Jesus, of course, was of the tribe of Judah because of his adoption by Joseph, "and no one from that tribe has ever served at the altar" (v. 13), and "Moses said nothing about priests" from Judah (v. 14). Conclusion? We need a new covenant—one that will have a priest in the order of Melchizedek serving at a greater tabernacle, based on greater sacrifices.

We are then given several reasons why the high priesthood of Jesus is superior, some of which we have already heard in Hebrews, plus a couple of additional reasons. Why a new priesthood? In 7:15–16 we are told that it is very clear why, because "another priest like Melchizedek appears, one who has become a priest not on the basis of a regulation as to his ancestry but on the basis of the power of an indestructible life." What an awesome thought! Jesus has an indestructible life, and therefore we can as well, through his mediation for us. The word for indestructible is *akatalytos,* which literally means unstoppable. When Jesus' life was taken on the cross, Satan may have thought he was destroyed, but Jesus has an unstoppable life. He was resurrected and has ascended to take his place as a priest forever. The permanence of the priesthood of Jesus is mentioned several times in Hebrews 7 alone. He is a priest forever (vv. 3, 17, 21), he is declared to be living (v. 8), his life is indestructible (v. 16), he has a permanent priesthood (v. 24), he is able to save completely (v. 25), he always lives (v. 25) and he is perfect forever (v. 28). We can be totally confident, because our high priest is on duty representing us to the Father 24/7 for eternity.

To complete the thought, let us go to verses 23 through 25: "Now there have been many of those priests [in the order of Levi], since death prevented them from continuing in office." Josephus, the Jewish historian, tells us that there were eighty-three high priests from the time of Aaron to the destruction of Jerusalem in AD 70. If we were putting our hopes in one of these priests, our hopes would have been dashed many times over, "but because Jesus lives forever, he has a permanent priesthood. Therefore he is able to save completely those who come to God through him, because he always lives to intercede for them." Here the word completely is *panteles,* which means complete, perfect, absolute. Please, take the time right now to contemplate how secure we are with Jesus as our intercessor—one who saves us absolutely. "For there is one God and one mediator between God and mankind, the man Christ Jesus" (1 Timothy 2:5).

There is another reason we needed a new covenant. "The former regulation is set aside because it was weak and useless" (v. 18). Useless? Really? These are strong words that might just get a Christian who has been going back to relying on Judaism angry, but they are true. We can admit that the old covenant was weak, but surely the law of Moses had some use. Paul gives us an idea of its usefulness, which is that "through the commandment sin might become utterly sinful" (Romans 7:13). In what sense, then, was the law "useless"? The law of Moses made nothing and no one perfect (v. 19). Isn't that what the law should do? We will see that the first covenant was only about outward regulations, which is why it made nothing perfect. Here the stage is being set for the argument that will be made in Hebrews 8 that the new covenant is undeniably superior to the old.

Besides, the new priesthood comes with an oath (v. 20). Priests in the order of Levi did not take oaths. The reason is that they surely would have broken any oath they made almost as soon as they took it. God is really trying to get our attention, because he tells us for the third time that "the Lord has sworn and will not change his mind: 'You are a priest forever'" (v. 21). God rarely makes an oath. He makes only three oaths in all of Scripture, and all of them relate to the current discussion:

1. **To Abraham about his descendants in Genesis 22**

2. **Concerning the coming priest in the order of Melchizedek in Psalm 110**

3. **To us about our salvation being sure in Hebrews 6:13–20**

Hopefully by now, even if we have minds that are nothros, God is starting to get through to us. Then our author repeats the argument of priesthood first and covenant second. He says, "Because of this oath [concerning the priesthood of Melchizedek], Jesus has become the guarantor [or pledge] of a better covenant" (v. 22).

God is almost through with his argument for the superiority of Jesus as a high priest and is about to go on to a discussion of the greatness of the covenant promises we have in Christ, but just in case there is the slightest chance we have not gotten it yet, he repeats one more time why Jesus is a perfect high priest.

> *Such a high priest truly meets our need—one who is holy, blameless, pure, set apart from sinners, exalted above the heavens. Unlike the other high priests, he does not need to offer sacrifices day after day, first for his own sins, and then for the sins of the people. He sacrificed for their sins once for all when he offered himself. For the law appoints as high priests men in all their weakness; but the oath, which came after the law, appointed the Son, who has been made perfect forever.* (Hebrews 7:26–28)

Jesus is not just a great high priest, he is a perfect one. Almost everything here has already been said and commented on or will be discussed in greater detail in a later chapter. This is a majestic summary of the greatness of Jesus as high priest. However, there is one important new idea we can glean from verse 27. Here we see that in the new covenant Jesus is both the priest who offers the sacrifice, and he is the sacrifice: "He offered himself." What a wonderful high priest! The high priests under the old covenant made sacrifices of animals. According to the regulation in Leviticus 16:6, the high priest had to pay for the bull that was offered for his own sins. Therefore, the high priest did have some skin in the game, as they say, but it did not cost him a whole lot to make the sacrifice on the Day of Atonement. It was an arduous task to make the sacrifices on Yom Kippur, and we can assume that the priests made the sacrifices with great fear for their own safety, but still, the personal cost to the Levitical high priest was not great. This is so different from our perfect and eternal high priest Jesus. What did he offer? Himself! This sacrifice cost the priest a lot—everything he had—his very life.

Hopefully our Jewish friends will forgive our use of this analogy, but perhaps you have heard the story of the chicken and the pig discussing the cost of breakfast the next day. The chicken boasts what a great sacrifice she is making by giving up one of her eggs to feed the family. The pig, however, is not all that impressed by the "sacrifice" of the chicken because in order to produce bacon, the pig must sacrifice everything.

Chapter 11

Jesus Is the Author of a Better Covenant
Hebrews 8:1–13

Chapter 8 is the shortest chapter in Hebrews, but there is a lot here for us to chew on. The principle point made in this section of the book is that the covenant established by Jesus is far superior to the former covenant made with Moses at Sinai. The greatness of the Christian covenant is based on the perfect high priesthood of Jesus, as we learned in Hebrews 7.

We have already considered in much detail what a priest is and the nature of priesthood, both to the ancient world in general and to the Jews more specifically. It is time to think carefully about the idea of covenant. In its broadest terms, a covenant is a solemn agreement between two or more parties. Merriam-Webster defines it as "a usually formal, solemn, and binding agreement." There are two words in Greek that are translated into English as "covenant." One of them is the more common of the two, which is *suntheke*. This was the term applied by Greek society to marriage covenants and to nearly all contracts, as well as diplomatic agreements between governments. It is the term used to describe a mutual agreement between parties. In other words, two or more come together, agree on a set of terms and go through whatever ceremony is required in the local culture to establish this agreement between the parties.

Even though it is the most common word for a covenant in Greek, the word *suntheke* is not used in Hebrews. Instead, a more specialized Greek term is used: *diatheke*. The term *diatheke* applies to a covenant that issues from one party in the situation but is binding on all. The most common use of the word *diatheke* is in the case of a will. In fact, in Hebrews 8 the word "will" could have been used in place of covenant in verses 7 through 10 and in verse 13. A will is a binding covenant on a group of people, but one that comes entirely at the initiative of one person. Also, the will or covenant does not come into effect until the one who created it dies. The new covenant is a *diatheke*. It is, in effect, a will established by God and put into effect on the death of his Son Jesus. Let us look for a moment at Hebrews 9:16–18:

> In the case of a will, it is necessary to prove the death of the one who made it, because a will is in force only when somebody has died; it never takes effect while the one who made it is living. This is why even the first covenant was not put into effect without blood. When Moses had proclaimed every command of the law to all the people, he took the blood of calves, together with water, scarlet wool and branches of hyssop, and sprinkled the scroll and all the people.

The Greek word translated as "will" in Hebrews 9:16 is *diatheke*. Both the old and the new covenant were put into force by blood, on the death of a sacrifice. When the new covenant came into place, it wholly replaced the covenant that had been established with the Jews at Sinai. And the covenant in blood established by the death of Jesus is truly a superior one. Let us turn to the text in chapter 8.

> Now the main point of what we are saying is this: We do have such a high priest, who sat down at the right hand of the throne of the Majesty in heaven, and who serves in the sanctuary, the true tabernacle set up by the Lord, not by a mere human being.
>
> Every high priest is appointed to offer both gifts and sacrifices, and so it was necessary for this one also to have something to offer. If he were on earth, he would not be a priest, for there are already priests who offer the gifts prescribed by the law. They serve at a sanctuary that is a copy and shadow of what is in heaven. This is why Moses was warned when he was about to build the tabernacle: "See to it that you make everything according to the pattern shown you on the mountain." But in fact the ministry Jesus has received is as superior to theirs as the covenant of which he is mediator is superior to the old one, since the new covenant is established on better promises. (Hebrews 8:1–6)

We are going to have to take just a short digression before we discuss covenants, in order for the writer of Hebrews to make a couple of comments about the priesthood and the tabernacle. What is the writer's main point here? Well, he told us, so we would do well to let him speak. The main point in the entire middle section of Hebrews—chapters 7 through 10—is that Jesus is our perfect high priest. This is based on the fact that the tabernacle he dwells in is superior; and it is because of his priesthood that we have a superior covenant and better sacrifices.

One reason we know that Jesus is so much greater than the Jewish high priest is that in the heavenly tabernacle he is seated at the right hand of God. What might seem a small point to a Gentile—that Jesus is seated—is something a Jew would certainly not miss. The priests were not allowed to sit when ministering in the tabernacle, or later in the temple. There were no chairs there except, of course, for the mercy seat. Who sits in the tabernacle? God does. The mercy seat, on the top of the ark of the covenant, is the place where God "sits." It is his throne. Priests must stand when in the sanctuary, because he is God and they are not. But Jesus, our high priest, is seated at the right hand of the throne of heaven. What a marvelous high priest we have in Jesus! He is our Lord and our God. (John 20:28)

Where does Jesus serve? He serves in the real thing, in the only tabernacle that really matters—the one where God's throne is. By comparison, as awesome as it is, the earthly temple is just "a copy and a shadow of what is in heaven." Please take some time right now to read Revelation 4:1–11 and picture in your mind God on his throne, and then look at Revelation 5:1–14 and get a vision of Jesus seated at his right hand. This is what we are talking about.

And notice this: What is Jesus doing in the real tabernacle, the heavenly one? He is serving. He is not ruling, although he certainly has the right to do so. Who is he serving? Who is he ministering to? He is serving you and me. He is *our* high priest. He is mediating on our behalf. Does that give you reason for confidence and joy?

We are reminded that the tabernacle where Jesus is serving as our mediator right now is not some ordinary building. It is not made by human hands. By the way, although the tabernacle was a portable building, something like a very fancy tent, it was beautiful and required vast wealth to build. The temple constructed by Solomon was considered the most beautiful and impressive building in the world. Of course, that was the opinion of the Jews, and they may have been a bit biased, but this was one amazing sanctuary. But let us be real about this building: it was built by human hands. Surely there were little mistakes in the weaving of the curtain, and the cylindrical columns were not perfect cylinders. There were imperfections in the tabernacle as well as in the temple, but the tabernacle where Jesus ministers on our behalf is supernaturally perfect.

Jesus did not serve in the earthly tabernacle, because at the time Hebrews was written, there were priests already appointed to that office serving in the sanctuary in Jerusalem. We are told that "if he were on earth, he would not be a priest." This seems a bit surprising. Wasn't Jesus a priest even while on the earth? To get an understanding of what the author is saying, consider that Jesus said of himself in John 12:47, "For I did not come to judge the world, but to save the world." Well, isn't Jesus a judge? Yes he is, but he did not come in the flesh to judge. His role as judge will come later. Isn't Jesus a priest? Yes, but he did not come in the flesh to serve as a priest. He took on that role after he gave his blood to establish the new covenant.

One of the important roles of the Aaronic priests was "to offer both gifts and sacrifices." The author of Hebrews is not repeating himself. Priests brought two qualitatively different things: gifts and sacrifices. The gifts, also known as offerings, included the burnt offering (*olah*, Leviticus 1), the grain offering (*minchah,* Leviticus 2), the drink offering (*nesek,* Leviticus 23:13) and the fellowship offering (*shelem,* Leviticus 7:11–15). These gifts were given as acts of worship. They were "an aroma pleasing to the Lord" (Leviticus 1:17). They had nothing to do with atonement. In fact, in the drink and grain offering, blood was not even involved. The gifts are mentioned here in Hebrews 8:3–4 and in 9:9, but they do not play an important part in Hebrews. The sacrifices, however, are key to the book. They were for sins committed, either against God or against fellow humans. They included the sin offering (chatat, Leviticus 4:1–5:13), the guilt offering (*asham*, Leviticus 5:14–6:7) and the red heifer sacrifice (Numbers 19). These sacrifices definitely did not produce a pleasing aroma, as they smelled of sin. Often they were burned outside the camp. They will be discussed in detail in the chapter on Hebrews 9:12–10:18.

The point in this passage is not what the priests bring, but the nature of where they serve. The Levitical priests served in a sanctuary that was merely a copy and shadow. We could distill the entire central section of Hebrews down using these two words. Every aspect of Judaism—its tabernacle, its gifts and its sacrifices—are mere copies and shadows of the reality we have in Christ.

The word translated "copy" is *hupodeigma.* It could be translated as "sketch," "plan" or "diorama." Do you remember those little models you made out of a shoe box when you were a child? They were called dioramas.

Maybe you made a model of the pilgrims or of Generals Lee and Grant (for those who are not from the USA, please forgive my colloquial examples). You put little plastic figures there and tiny pretend guns or pumpkins or whatever to set the scene. This is what the tabernacle or temple where the Jews worshipped was like. In the Jerusalem Museum there is a famous scale model of the ancient city that many tourists visit while in the ancient Jewish capital. It is an artist's representation of Jerusalem in the first century. Imagine traveling all the way to Jerusalem only to go and see the scale model, but never actually touring the city. That would be a waste of time. This is what the Jewish form of worship is like compared to the reality we have in Christ. Believe it or not, some of the Jewish Christians were going back to relying on the diorama. We could do the same thing if we rely on our religious actions or our works or even on our church to maintain our relationship with God. Where do you find your security—in Jesus or in religious things?

The second word used here to describe the Jewish tabernacle is *skia*. This word can mean shadow, reflection or silhouette. Greek writers such as Plato often used the metaphor of the shadow or reflection. They described this physical world as a mere shadow, but the heavens as the greater reality. This idea was familiar to the audience of Hebrews. What does a shadow weigh? What is a silhouette made of? Shadows have no color and they are only two-dimensional. Imagine someone coming up to you and talking to your shadow rather than talking to you. That would be truly bizarre, and it also would look very foolish. This is what it is like to base our relationship with God on things of the world or on religious ceremony. This is what the Jewish Christians to whom Hebrews was addressed were beginning to do. As we will see in Hebrews 10:1, "the law is only a shadow of the good things that are coming—not the realities themselves." The law of Moses and the regulations prescribed in the law, as well as the festivals and the sacrifices, are all only foreshadows of the things we have in Christ. Everything in Judaism was just preparing the way so that when the real thing came, we could immediately turn our attention from the shadow to the reality. So, let us take our eyes off the shadow; let us not waste our time contemplating the diorama. Let us look to Jesus.

Because the tabernacle was, in essence, a scale model of the real tabernacle, "this is why Moses was warned when he was about to make the tabernacle and its accessories, 'See to it that you make them according to the pattern shown you on the mountain'" (Exodus 25:40). The mountain, of course, is Sinai. Why was it so important that Moses make the tabernacle precisely according to the instructions? Because it was a model of something that was holy and perfect. The attention to details was a reminder both of what it was not (perfect) and of what the tabernacle was a copy of—perfection itself. The most boring section of the entire Bible just might be Ezekiel 40–46, in which God gives Ezekiel a vision of the heavenly temple. In these chapters God goes into almost infinite detail about every conceivable aspect of this temple, down to the width of the porticos (what is a portico?) and the height of the alcoves. Why all the details of a temple that was never actually built?

> Son of man, describe the temple to the people of Israel, that they may be ashamed of their sins. Let them consider its perfection, and if they are ashamed of all they have done, make known to them the design of the temple—its arrangement, its exits and entrances—its whole design and all its regulations and laws. (Ezekiel 43:10–11a)

Most of us will have to admit that when we read this section of Ezekiel, we do not find ourselves immediately thinking about how sinful we are, but we should. We need to consider the implications of God's perfection, of his design and of his arrangement for our salvation, and we should be convicted of our sinfulness and come to Jesus, the pioneer and perfecter of our salvation.

Now we are ready for our main point in chapter 8: "But in fact the ministry Jesus has received is as superior to theirs as the covenant of which he is a mediator is superior to the old one, since the new covenant is established on better promises." Jesus ministers to us in a perfect sanctuary, offering perfect gifts and sacrifices to a perfect God. Just as the earthly sanctuary does not hold a candle to this, in the same way, the new covenant can be compared to the covenant of Moses. It is like comparing a stick figure you or I could draw to the Mona Lisa. It is like comparing a cockroach (sorry, cockroaches!) to a human being. We have an amazing covenant, so why would you go back to the former? In what ways is the covenant established by the death of Jesus superior?

> For if there had been nothing wrong with that first covenant, no place would have been sought for another. But God found fault with the people and said:
>
> "The days are coming, declares the Lord,

when I will make a new covenant
with the people of Israel
    and with the people of Judah.
It will not be like the covenant
    I made with their ancestors
when I took them by the hand
    to lead them out of Egypt,
because they did not remain faithful to my covenant,
    and I turned away from them,
    declares the Lord.
This is the covenant I will establish with the people of
Israel
    after that time, declares the Lord.
I will put my laws in their minds
    and write them on their hearts.
I will be their God,
    and they will be my people.
No longer will they teach their neighbor,
    or say to one another, 'Know the Lord,'
because they will all know me,
    from the least of them to the greatest.
For I will forgive their wickedness
    and will remember their sins no more."
By calling this covenant "new" he has made the first
one obsolete; and what is obsolete and outdated will soon
disappear. (Hebrews 8:7–13)

"Houston, we have a problem..." There was a problem with the old covenant. What was the problem? We were the problem: "But God found fault with the people." As God said to his people, "The person who does these things will live by them" (Leviticus 18:5; Romans 10:5). But we did not do those things. "All have sinned and fall short of the glory of God" (Romans 3:23). "There is no one righteous, not even one" (Psalm 14:3; Romans 3:10). Not only do all sin, but "it is impossible for the blood of bulls and goats to take away sins" (Hebrews 10:4). This was not a good situation.

All true, but God gives us great news in Jeremiah 31:31–34, quoted here. This is the longest Old Testament quote in the New Testament, and it is one of the most significant prophecies in the Bible. Despite the fact that "they did not remain faithful to my covenant," God planned all along to give a new covenant—one that was far superior to the old. There are several reasons the Christian covenant is greater. Here are just a few:

1. **It is based on better promises.**

2. **It is based on the righteousness of Jesus rather than on our own righteousness (which is dubious anyway).**

3. **We serve God because we want to, not out of obligation.**

4. **It is a personal relationship—not one mediated by another human.**

5. **Under this covenant there is real and lasting forgiveness.**

God promises us, "I will put my laws in their minds and write them on their hearts." We will obey God because it is on our hearts. We will have the will and the desire to do what he says. The reason this is the case is that in the new covenant, the obligation to perfectly follow law has been canceled. God "canceled the charge of our legal indebtedness" (Colossians 2:14). "It is for freedom that Christ has set us free" (Galatians 5:1); and obligation to the law is what we have been set free from. It is so much better to serve God because we love him rather than out of duty, under which one violation brings punishment and condemnation. In Christ, "the only thing that counts is faith expressing itself through love" (Galatians 5:6). If the Christ has set us free [from obligation], then we are free indeed (paraphrasing John 8:36). As God prophesied through Ezekiel, "I will give them an undivided heart and put a new spirit in them; I will remove from them their heart of stone and give them a heart of flesh" (Ezekiel 11:19). This is a much better covenant.

In Jeremiah 31 and Hebrews 8 God promises us that "I will be their God, and they will be my people." And "they will all know me." This is one of those "better promises" of Hebrews 8:6. The relationship we have with God through our mediator and high priest Jesus is a personal one. As was prophesied in Hosea 2:23, "I will say to those called 'Not my people,' 'You are my people'; and they will say, 'You are my God.'" The book of Hosea is one of the most beautiful depictions of the kind of relationship we can have with God through Jesus. We are family. We are friends. We belong. All of this is found in Christ and in his covenant.

Best of all, God will forgive our wickedness, and our sins will no longer be called to mind. We have freedom, not only from obligation, but from the horrible, debilitating, devastating, damning effects of our sin. What a stupendous covenant we have.

The covenant with Moses is the foreshadow, and the covenant through Jesus is what is anticipated in the foreshadow. The old covenant is the type, and the new covenant is the antitype. The general pattern is that things in the law of Moses involve the physical, while the real things, the things in the new covenant, are similar but spiritual. A few examples of this principle are in the table below.

Prefigure in the Law of Moses	*Realization in the Law of Christ*
Obedience to physically defined rules	Obedience to spiritual principles
Physical blessings promised	Spiritual blessings promised
Ceremonial uncleanness removed	Sin removed
Sacrifice bridges the chasm between law and effort	Sacrifice bridges the chasm between law and effort
Sealed with the blood of bulls and goats	Sealed with the blood of Jesus
Mediated by an imperfect high priest	Mediated by the perfect high priest, Jesus Christ
Laws, rules and regulations for behavior	Obedience based on love
Tithing	Sacrificing from the heart
Sabbath	Come...I will give you rest—relying on Jesus
Death	Life

One would think that, given the infinite advantages gained through Christ, no sane person would go back to relying on the law, but this is something that the Christians addressed in Hebrews were doing. Or at least they were sorely tempted to do so. If it could happen to them, it could happen to us. Actually, what would happen to us is the Gentile equivalent of relying on the ceremonies and laws in the Old Testament; we too can rely on outward acts. We can return from true discipleship to Jesus to a safe and comfortable religiosity. Therefore, the writer of Hebrews feels the need to tell us one more time: "By calling this covenant 'new,' he has made the first one obsolete; and what is obsolete and outdated will soon disappear." We are told that the shadow, the scale model, the old covenant, is obsolete and outdated. It is like milk that is a couple of weeks past its freshness date. It is time for new milk. When Jesus died, the curtain in the temple that separated the holy place from the holy of holies was torn in two from top to bottom (Matthew 27:51). This was no mere symbolic occurrence. We will see in Hebrews 10 that it has great positive significance for us as Christians. Clearly, it was an act of God.

Why did he rend the curtain in two, and what was the result? We are not told directly in Matthew, but we can reasonably infer that when the curtain was torn, God's presence left the temple. This would be reminiscent of what happened in Ezekiel 10:18–19 and 11:22–24. Because of the sin of the people, God withdrew himself from the temple built by Solomon in which he had dwelt for more than three hundred and fifty years. When he left the temple, God had, in a sense, abandoned his people. It was just a matter of time before the prophecies in Ezekiel were fulfilled, as Nebuchadnezzar entered the city and burned the temple to the ground in 586 BC.

In AD 30 God's presence left the second temple. At that point, it became an empty shell. Gifts and sacrifices were still offered, but to a God who no longer dwelt in the temple. As was said earlier, most likely Hebrews was written in the mid to late 60s. At that time, the Jewish system of sacrifice was old and fading, as the Hebrew writer said to his audience. As already mentioned, in AD 70 Roman General and future Emperor Titus entered the city of Jerusalem and burned the temple to the ground, offering pagan sacrifice on the temple site. What was old and fading did "disappear" in AD 70, and the temple has never been rebuilt. It never will be. The sacrificial system established at Sinai is no longer practiced, even by those who remain Jews. Let us not rely on our own righteous deeds; let us fix our eyes on Jesus. Let us come to God based on a new and much better covenant.

End Notes _____

8. God did not fully abandoned his chosen people until AD 70. Even then, they were not truly abandoned, because they already had access to him through the blood of Jesus and had since AD 30. That God never abandoned his people is established by many Old Testament passages, but we will use Malachi 1:1–2, where God responds to the people when they question his continuous love. "'Was not Esau Jacob's brother?' declares the Lord. 'Yet I have loved Jacob'" (i.e. Israel)

___ Chapter 12 ___

Jesus Dwells in a Greater, Heavenly Tabernacle
Hebrews 9:1–11

The purpose of Hebrews 9:1–11 is to establish the superiority of the tabernacle where Jesus dwells over the earthly tabernacle, which was merely a copy, a shadow, a diorama of the true one where Jesus ministers to us as our heavenly high priest. In chapter 8, the tabernacle and the sacrifices are mentioned, but the main subject is covenant. Similarly, in this section, covenant and sacrifices are mentioned, but the tabernacle is the chief topic.

> *Now the first covenant had regulations for worship and also an earthly sanctuary. A tabernacle was set up. In its first room were the lampstand and the table with its consecrated bread; this was called the Holy Place. Behind the second curtain was a room called the Most Holy Place, which had the golden altar of incense and the gold-covered ark of the covenant. This ark contained the gold jar of manna, Aaron's staff that had budded, and the stone tablets of the covenant. Above the ark were the cherubim of the Glory, overshadowing the atonement cover. But we cannot discuss these things in detail now.* (Hebrews 9:1–5)

Remember that this is a written-down sermon. The "preacher" does not have time to discuss all of the items in the tabernacle and their significance. Besides, his audience is primarily Jewish, so telling them about the tabernacle would be like telling someone from Mexico about the game of soccer. What the author of Hebrews does not have time for, and does not have need to do, we will do. Let us consider in some detail the items in the tabernacle and later in the temple, and their meaning as foreshadows of the reality we have in Christ.

First, it should be noted that the writer of Hebrews speaks at length about the tabernacle, the portable sanctuary that the Jews carried with them as they moved through the wilderness, but pointedly never mentions the temple. Most likely, this is because he does not want to draw undue attention to the temple, toward which the Jewish Christians are already being tempted to put too much devotion. Also, the tabernacle is the sanctuary whose pattern is actually specified in the law of Moses. The details of the design of the tabernacle are found in Exodus 25–31 and 35–40.

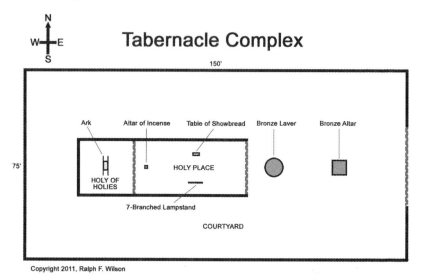

Copyright 2011, Ralph F. Wilson

The tabernacle was surrounded by an outer curtain of white linen, which was approximately fifty meters by twenty-five meters. The white of the linen symbolized the holiness of the sanctuary. There was a single opening in this curtain/fence, which faced to the east. When Israel camped in the wilderness, three of the tribes camped to the east, three to the north, three to the west and three to the south of the tabernacle. When God occupied the tabernacle, there was a cloud by day and a pillar of fire at night. God literally dwelt among his people in the wilderness, which has great significance when we consider that in John 1:14 we are told that Jesus came and "made his dwelling" (literally, tabernacled) among us.

In Solomon's as well as in Herod's temple, the court of the Levites was entered through a larger court of the (Jewish) men, which was, in turn, entered through a court for the (Jewish) women, which was surrounded by an even more distant court for the Gentiles. All of this symbolized, not the access to God that we had outside of Christ, but how distant and how separated we were from God until our perfect high priest Jesus gave us access to him.

The Jewish people were not allowed inside the outer fence into the courtyard of the tabernacle. Only the Levites and the priests were allowed into the courtyard. It was in this open section that the altar of sacrifice and the laver were found. God dwelt in the most holy place, which was entered by first passing through the holy place. But in order for a priest to enter the holy place, he must first make sacrifice at the altar and clean himself at the laver. Remember that every single object in the tabernacle serves as a foreshadow of how we as Christians gain access to God, who dwells in the real holy of holies, where Jesus ministers. The symbolic meaning of the altar of sacrifice (also known as the brazen altar because it was sheathed in bronze) and of the laver and their New Testament equivalents is not hard to see. In order for us to gain access to God, the first requirement is a sacrifice. For us, of course, this is the sacrifice of Jesus. The sin and guilt offerings were made on the altar in the courtyard. Is the sacrifice of Jesus sufficient to gain access to the presence of God? Some might say so, but it was required that all priests must first wash in the laver: "Whenever they enter the tent of meeting [i.e., the holy place], they shall wash with water so that they will not die" (Exodus 30:20). The symbolism of the laver is clear. It is a foreshadow of baptism, which a disciple of Jesus must undergo in order to receive forgiveness of sins, the indwelling Holy Spirit (Acts 2:38–39) and, therefore, access to the heavenly tabernacle. Only priests could wash in the laver, and all Christians are priests (Exodus 19:6; 1 Peter 2:9).

Having made a sacrifice at the altar and washed at the laver, the priest was ready to enter the holy place. He would pass into the holy place through a curtain made of linen dyed blue, purple and scarlet, which were symbolic of heaven, royalty and blood. This area was rectangular in shape, about five meters tall and wide, and ten meters long. On the right was the table with the shewbread, which was a foreshadow of Jesus, who is the bread of life. On the left was the menorah or golden lampstand with seven lamps. The lampstand is a foreshadow of the Holy Spirit (Zechariah 4:2–6). The third object in the holy place was the altar of incense. It lay directly in front of the curtain that separated the holy place from the holy of holies. The altar of incense is symbolic of the prayers of the saints (Revelation 8:3–4). The fact that the curtain separated the altar of incense from the holy of holies is one more symbol, which represents that before the death of Christ, our prayers did not have direct access to the Father. It is difficult to know why the writer of Hebrews describes the altar of incense as being in the most holy place in Hebrews 9:3–4, as it was certainly just in front of the curtain. This is clear from Exodus 30:6. The altar was placed "in front of the curtain" so that some of the fragrance of the incense burned on it could penetrate the curtain and enter the presence of God. Aaron and his successors burned incense on the altar every day (Exodus 30:7), which provides further evidence that it was in front of the veil. Surely some of the smoke from the incense burned there did enter the holy of holies, which may be what our author has in mind, but the actual altar was in front of the curtain.

This curtain, which symbolized our separation from God, like the curtain at the entrance to the holy place, was made of blue, purple and scarlet linen. On the curtain were embroidered figures of cherubim. The cherubim are the angels who kept Adam and Eve from accessing the Garden of Eden. They are around God's throne, protecting his holiness (Revelation 4:6–9; Ezekiel 1:4–14). A sinful person would do well to stay away from the cherubim!

In the most holy place was the ark of the covenant. Inside the ark were a golden jar of manna, Aaron's rod and the two tablets on which Moses received the Ten Commandments. The mercy seat was the cover on the ark. Symbolically, the mercy seat "covers" the law of Moses, as it represents God's mercy, which replaces law. God's presence was over the mercy seat, between two golden statues of cherubim. It was on the mercy seat that the high priest sprinkled blood from the sacrificial bull and the goat on the Day of Atonement. A summary of the items in the tabernacle and their meaning as foreshadows is in the table below.

Item in the Tabernacle or Temple	Antitype in the New Covenant	Scripture Reference
The tabernacle itself	God dwelling with his people	John 14:1–3, 1:14; Revelation 1:13
The bronze altar of sacrifice	The sacrifice of Jesus for or sins	Hebrews 9:14
The basin/laver	Baptism	Titus 3:5
The show bread	The bread of life, Jesus	John 6:48–51
The lampstand	The Holy Spirit	Zechariah 4:2–6
The altar of incense	Prayers of the saints	Revelation 5:8
The blue, purple and scarlet yarn	The heavens, the kingship of God, the blood of Jesus	
The curtain	Separation from God	Matthew 27:51
The ark of the covenant	The presence of God	Psalm 132:7–8
The mercy seat	The grace of God	Psalm 99:1
The cherubim	Protecting God's holiness	Ezekiel 10:15–22

Truly the tabernacle was a magnificent structure—sufficiently beautiful and sacred that God could dwell in the holy of holies. But just as there was something "wrong" with the first covenant (Hebrews 8:7), there was something wrong with the tabernacle. It was merely a scale model of the real, heavenly tabernacle and, besides, it represented separation from God at least as much as it represented access to him.

When everything had been arranged like this, the priests entered regularly into the outer room to carry on their ministry. But only the high priest entered the inner room, and that only once a year, and never without blood, which he offered for himself and for the sins the people had committed in ignorance. The Holy Spirit was showing by this that the way into the Most Holy Place had not yet been disclosed as long as the first tabernacle was still functioning. This is an illustration for the present time, indicating that the gifts and sacrifices being offered were not able to clear the conscience of the worshiper. They are only a matter of food and drink and various ceremonial washings—external regulations applying until the time of the new order.

But when Christ came as high priest of the good things that are now already here, he went through the greater and more perfect tabernacle that is not made with human hands, that is to say, is not a part of this creation. (Hebrews 9:6–11)

We have already seen, in the chapter on Hebrews 4:14–5:10, that a chief function of the high priest was to enter the most holy place once a year to make a sacrifice of atonement for the sins of the people. And we are reminded here that this sacrifice was not for willful sin, but only for sins committed "in ignorance." Unfortunately, this is not the only kind of sin we need atonement for! All of us have committed uncountable willful, rebellious acts against the holiness of God. The Jewish high priests could not help us there. We learn a few more things here that point to the weakness and inefficacy of the sacrifices made by the high priests in the order of Aaron. They did not give us access to the Holy of Holies—not even to the copy, never mind the real one. The way had "not yet been disclosed." That is a big drawback, to put it mildly. As long as the tabernacle (or the temple) was functioning, access to God was not available. Fortunately for us, when Jesus died and the curtain was rent in two, the tabernacle/temple ceased to function, and at that time we gained access to the presence of God, though not through Herod's temple.

There is more. The Holy Spirit is telling us here that this is an illustration (Greek: *parabole,* illustration, parable, figure of speech) that the gifts and sacrifices in the law of Moses did not clear our consciences. This is not surprising. Which bothers our consciences more, the sins we committed in ignorance, or the ones we committed willfully? Besides, even if our consciences deceived us and we felt clear of guilt, there remained the fact that our sins were not forgiven.

Why were our consciences still feeling guilty? Because we were still guilty! The gifts and sacrifices outlined in Leviticus were "only a matter of food and drink and various ceremonial washings—external regulations applying until the time of the new order." This revelation about the law of Moses is devastating! It only involved outward things. The sacrifices in the covenant with Moses only created ceremonial cleanness. In other words, they did not remove sin. They were only a stopgap measure so that the Jews could worship God without being destroyed by him. The law of Moses was great, the sacrifices were amazing, and the tabernacle was impressive, but when we consider what we have in Christ, they pale by comparison.

Are you ready for some truly astonishing, life-changing news? "But when Christ came as high priest of the good things that are now already here, he went through the greater and more perfect tabernacle that is not made with human hands, that is to say, is not part of this creation." Some of the "buts" in the Bible are followed by bad news, but this is not one of them. Through his better sacrifice, Christ is mediating for us in a much better tabernacle. He is serving our interests and speaking for us in a perfect tabernacle—one that, unlike the Jewish tabernacle, is not made with human hands and has no imperfections. Folks, this is the real thing. It is the tabernacle in which we get access to God.

What a great tabernacle this is! It is the place where God dwells, not only in a limited sense, as he did in the tabernacle in the wilderness. Here we get unfettered access to our Father in heaven. The wooden posts that held up the superstructure of the temple eventually decomposed or perhaps were eaten by termites. Over time, the curtains were eaten by moths. But this, the tabernacle that Jesus entered, is not part of this creation. This creation is good—it is very good (Genesis 1:31)—but it is not eternal, and it is not perfect. Truly the tabernacle where Jesus serves is a greater one.

___ Chapter 13 ___

Jesus Offers a Greater Sacrifice
Hebrews 9:12–10:18

I f Hebrews chapter 7 is the heart of the argument made in the book, then Hebrews 9:12–10:18 is the culmination and the pinnacle of what we are learning about the greatness of our high priest Jesus. It is not the covenant that saves us. It is not the tabernacle that saves us. It is the sacrifice that saves us and makes us at one with God, and the sacrifice of Jesus is of immeasurably greater value than all the sacrifices in the old covenant.

Hebrews 9:12–14 is one of the most elegant and moving passages in the book.

> He did not enter by means of the blood of goats and calves; but he entered the Most Holy Place once for all by his own blood, thus obtaining eternal redemption. The blood of goats and bulls and the ashes of a heifer sprinkled on those who are ceremonially unclean sanctify them so that they are outwardly clean. How much more, then, will the blood of Christ, who through the eternal Spirit offered himself unblemished to God, cleanse our consciences from acts that lead to death, so that we may serve the living God!

The sacrifice of Jesus is so superior to anything in the law of Moses that there is almost no point in comparing them, yet compare them we will. In Hebrews 9:12–28 the comparison takes the form of a type/antitype analysis in which the Jewish Day of Atonement, Yom Kippur, is the type, and the sacrificial death of Jesus is the antitype. The argument began in Hebrews 9:11 when we were told, "But when Christ came as high priest of the good things that are now already here, he went through the greater and more perfect tabernacle that is not made with human hands, that is to say, is not a part of this creation." This verse connects the argument regarding the two tabernacles with the argument concerning the sacrifices. We have already seen a number of type/antitype relationships used in Hebrews. Moses is the type, and Jesus is the antitype, but he is much greater than Moses. Melchizedek is the type, and Jesus is the antitype, but his priesthood is vastly superior. The old covenant is the type, and the new covenant is the antitype, but the covenant in Christ is grander than the former. The earthly tabernacle is the type, and the heavenly tabernacle is the antitype, of which the former is only a scale model and a shadow.

The Day of Atonement is the type, and the high priestly sacrifice of Jesus is the antitype, but as with the other examples, the antitype is immeasurably greater in the benefit it brings to God's people. A few of the reasons are contained in the table below.

The Lesser Sacrifice (Goats, Bulls, Red Heifer)	The Greater Sacrifice (Jesus)
Outward (appearance)	Inward (spiritual)
Temporary (continually repeated)	Eternal (done only once)
Ceremonial	Real
Not voluntary	Voluntary
Mechanical	Spontaneous (by choice)
Unaware	Rational, aware

Why is the sacrifice of Jesus, like the tabernacle, "greater and more perfect?" First of all, because the blood of Jesus is much more effectual at atoning for sin than the "blood of goats and bulls." The blood of goats and bulls is a direct reference to the Day of Atonement. When the high priest entered the holy of holies to make atonement, he first went in with the blood of a young bull (the Hebrew word can mean a young bull or calf), sprinkling it seven times over the mercy seat. He then briefly came back out of the inner sanctuary and mingled together the blood of the calf with that of the sacrificial goat, returning to sprinkle the mixture seven times over the atonement cover.

Why does the blood of Christ speak better for us than that of bulls and goats? First, because it brings about "eternal redemption." Which is better, to have temporary redemption or eternal redemption? Would you rather have your guilt removed for one day or for eternity? If your guilt is only removed temporarily, was it really effectually removed? Another huge difference between the effect of the blood of Jesus and that of four-footed animals is that the blood of animals only created ceremonial cleanness. Under the former covenant, the outside was sufficiently clean so that the Jews could worship God without being destroyed, but the inside was still left corroded and thoroughly stained with sin. The blood of Christ makes us clean from sin both inside and out.

As we are told, the blood of Christ, unlike that of goats and calves, gives us a clear conscience. Let us ask ourselves a question. What would be of more value to you than having a conscience cleansed "from acts that lead to death?" Which is of more worth, a nice vacation home or a conscience as clean as the driven snow? Which would you pay more for, a brand new, stylish outfit to wear or the removal of a death sentence? This is how much greater the sacrifice of Jesus is than anything in the law of Moses.

We should not forget that Jesus was also an unblemished sacrifice. In this he was similar to, but greater than, the Jewish sacrifices. The lambs slain for the Passover, as well as the animals sacrificed on the Day of Atonement, had to be without physical blemish. Jesus also was without imperfections; he was human and suffered every temptation as we do, yet he remained spiritually unblemished. The type had to be physically unblemished. The antitype, being human, had to be spiritually unblemished. Which is more rare, to be physically unblemished or spiritually unblemished?

In verse 12, the blood of goats and calves is mentioned, whereas in verse 13, the blood of goats and bulls and the ashes of a heifer are listed as creating merely ceremonial cleanness. The type/antitype relationship between the Day of Atonement and the blood of Jesus is anticipated in both verses, but what about "the ashes of a heifer?" There is nothing about the ashes of a heifer in the description of the Day of Atonement. These ashes are a reference to another sacrifice, known as the red heifer sacrifice. Just so you know, a heifer is a young female cow, especially one that has not yet borne a calf.

There is no doubt that the writer of Hebrews includes the red heifer sacrifice, as this is the only possible thing in the Jewish sacrificial system to which he can be referring. At first, it seems strange to bring in what is a relatively obscure part of the sacrificial system when the subject is the type/antitype relationship between the Day of Atonement and the blood sacrifice of Jesus. The red heifer sacrifice is described in Numbers 19:1–22. It is interesting that it is not mentioned in Leviticus. Scholars believe it may well have predated the giving of the law at Sinai. The purpose of this sacrifice was to create ceremonial cleanness for those who had touched a dead body or another unclean object.

"Whoever touches a human corpse will be unclean for

seven days. They must purify themselves with the water [from the red heifer sacrifice] on the third day and on the seventh day; then they will be clean.... If they fail to purify themselves after touching a human corpse, they defile the LORD's tabernacle. They must be cut off from Israel. Because the water of cleansing has not been sprinkled on them, they are unclean; their uncleanness remains on them...anyone who touches a human bone or a grave, will be unclean for seven days.

"For the unclean person, put some ashes from the burned purification offering [i.e., from the red heifer sacrifice] into a jar and pour fresh water over them. Then a man who is ceremonially clean is to take some hyssop, dip it in the water, and sprinkle the tent and all the furnishings and the people who were there." (Numbers 19:11–13, 16–18)

The ashes used in this ceremonial purification were the remains of a red heifer that had been burned outside the camp. This was a special red heifer. It was required to be completely unblemished, with no more than three hairs on its entire body that were not red. It was required that it had never been yoked (Numbers 19:2). The entire heifer was burned. As it was burned, cedar wood, hyssop and scarlet wool were thrown into the fire.

This is all quite interesting, but it begs the question of why it warrants mention in Hebrews 9:13. The author does not tell us. Let us suggest two reasons why "the ashes of a heifer sprinkled on those who are ceremonially unclean" are mentioned in this context. First, this was the only sacrifice in the Old Testament that was used to purify both Jews and Gentiles. Anyone living among the Jews who touched a dead body or a bone or a grave could be made ceremonially clean through the red heifer sacrifice, and this included Gentiles. The blood of Christ atones for the sins of all—Jew and Gentile alike. The Day of Atonement was not for all, but the red heifer sacrifice was. That it is a sacrifice for all may be one of the reasons the Hebrew writer included it.

A second reason this relatively obscure sacrifice is mentioned may be that the parallels in the type/antitype relationship between the red heifer sacrifice and the death of Jesus are uncanny. Every detail of this sacrifice points to Jesus. A list of the parallels is in the table below.

Aspects of the Red Heifer Sacrifice	Antitype in the Sacrifice of Jesus
A very rare red heifer	A unique son
Sacrificed outside the camp	Sacrificed outside Jerusalem
Purifies both Jew and Gentile	Atones for the sin of both Jew and Gentile
A sacrifice without blemish	A sacrifice without sin
Had never been yoked	Offered himself voluntarily
Scarlet wool and wood included	Blood shed on a wooden cross
Hyssop included (for purification from the effects of death)	Purifies us from the effects of sin
Water included for purification	Baptized into Christ for forgiveness

The red heifer had never been yoked. This figuratively represents that it had never been led against its will. Similarly, Jesus was a rational and willing sacrifice. The red heifer was unique, or nearly so. The great medieval Jewish scholar Maimonides informs us that in the entire history of the Jews, only ten red heifers that met all of the qualifications were ever found.[9] The red heifer is nearly unique, and Jesus is unique; the one and only Son of God. The red heifer was unblemished. Jesus is without sin. Cedar wood; hyssop, which symbolized purification; and scarlet wool, which represents blood, were added to the sacrifice when it was burned. This is a figure of Jesus' blood, which was shed on a wooden cross and purifies us from sin. The heifer was burned outside the camp. Jesus was executed outside the city of Jerusalem. Many of the reasons the writer of Hebrews wants to give for why the sacrifice of Jesus is superior are illustrated by the parallels between the sacrifice of Jesus and the red heifer sacrifice. It takes about forty-five minutes to read Hebrews aloud, which is about the length of a typical sermon. There was not sufficient time for him to unpack the awesome parallels between the red heifer sacrifice and that of Jesus, but we are not constrained by time here. The sacrifice of Jesus is truly great.

"How much more, then, will the blood of Christ, who through the eternal Spirit offered himself unblemished to God, cleanse our consciences" (v. 14). Yes, indeed. How much more effective is the blood of Jesus! Another thing that makes his sacrifice superior is that Jesus "offered himself." This tells us two things about Jesus as a sacrifice that make this offering so much better than that of a sheep or a goat or a bull: his was a willing sacrifice, and his was a rational offering. If we were to ask the goat or bull for permission to take its life, first of all, the animal would not be able to understand the question. An animal is not a rational being, not self-aware as Jesus was. But even if we could somehow get through to the sheep so that it could understand what we were asking, surely the answer would be an emphatic "No! You do not have permission to take my life!" Which is a better sacrifice, one given willingly or one that is taken from a creature that is not even aware of what is going on and would refuse if it could be asked? In Isaiah 53:7 we are told about Jesus that "he was led like a lamb to the slaughter." In one sense Jesus was like the lamb, in that the sacrifice did not have to be forced to the slaughter. In another sense he is not like a sheep, because a sheep has no idea what is coming, but Jesus most certainly did, as he prayed, "My Father, if it is not possible for this cup to be taken away unless I drink it, may your will be done" (Matthew 26:42).

What is the result of this incredible sacrifice—the sacrifice of Jesus? Not only are we given eternally clean consciences, we are purified so that we may serve God (9:14). The purpose of the Jewish sacrifices was to create ceremonial cleanness so that the people could worship God without fear. The blood of Jesus has the same effect for us, but it does more. Through his sacrifice, we are made ministers of reconciliation (2 Corinthians 5:18). We are made clean so that we may serve God in the most important work in the universe, which is helping others come to know Christ. Without the blood of Christ, we are "unfit for doing anything good" (Titus 1:16). We really needed this sacrifice.

The writer of Hebrews has more to say about this greater sacrifice:

> For this reason Christ is the mediator of a new covenant, that those who are called may receive the promised eternal inheritance—now that he has died as a ransom to set them free from the sins committed under the first covenant.
>
> In the case of a will, it is necessary to prove the death of the one who made it, because a will is in force only when somebody has died; it never takes effect while the one who made it is living. This is why even the first covenant was not put into effect without blood. When Moses had proclaimed every command of the law to all the people, he took the blood of calves, together with water, scarlet wool and branches of hyssop, and sprinkled the scroll and all the people. He said, "This is the blood of the covenant, which God has commanded you to keep." In the same way, he sprinkled with the blood both the tabernacle and everything used in its ceremonies.

In fact, the law requires that nearly everything be cleansed with blood, and without the shedding of blood there is no forgiveness. (Hebrews 9:15–22)

The idea of a greater sacrifice is the main thought in this entire section, but our author returns for a moment to the superiority of the covenant put into effect by the blood of Jesus. This was the subject of Hebrews 8. One thing our author had not mentioned back in Hebrews 8 was the means by which a will or a covenant is put into effect. The sacrificial death of Jesus is the "ransom" that sets us free from the sins we have committed (v. 15), but it is also the means by which and the point in time at which the covenant goes into effect. We are reminded of something we probably already know, which is that "a will is in force only when somebody has died." Jesus' death ratifies the covenant, and it initiates him into his role as mediator on our behalf in the heavenly tabernacle.

In the ancient Near East, covenants were sealed by what would seem to us a bizarre ritual. In the ceremony, an animal or animals were sacrificed, their bodies were cut in half, and the ones agreeing to the covenant walked between the halves. The symbolic meaning was that whoever walked between the dismembered bodies invoked on themself the same fate if they were unfaithful to the covenant. This was a solemn ceremony. An example of this is found in Genesis 15:8–17. In a vision, God's covenant with Abraham is sealed by a torch passing between the divided bodies of a heifer, a goat and a ram, along with the bodies of a dove and pigeon left whole. The fact that only the torch and not Abraham passed between the separated corpses of the animals was symbolic that the covenant with Abraham, like the covenant sealed with the blood of Jesus, was made entirely by the action of God, not of Abraham. The point of mentioning this example is that for the Jews, a covenant is not sealed until the one ratifying it has bound himself to the covenant by means of a representative animal. In Hebrews 9:17 the expression could be translated more literally as "a covenant is confirmed over dead bodies."

The entire next paragraph could easily be condensed down to its final statement: "Without the shedding of blood there is no forgiveness." The first covenant established at Sinai was sealed with blood. Obviously, atonement at Yom Kippur was obtained by blood. Even the red heifer sacrifice, which, technically, did not involve blood, included scarlet wool, which symbolizes blood. No blood, no covenant. No blood, no forgiveness. Why? Because "the life of a creature is in the blood…it is the blood that makes atonement for one's life" (Leviticus 17:11).

With the greater sacrifice of Christ still in view, the writer of Hebrews moves on to a discussion of the tabernacle in the light of this sacrifice.

> *It was necessary, then, for the copies of the heavenly things to be purified with these sacrifices, but the heavenly things themselves with better sacrifices than these. For Christ did not enter a sanctuary made with human hands that was only a copy of the true one; he entered heaven itself, now to appear for us in God's presence. Nor did he enter heaven to offer himself again and again, the way the high priest enters the Most Holy Place every year with blood that is not his own. Otherwise Christ would have had to suffer many times since the creation of the world. But he has appeared once for all at the culmination of the ages to do away with sin by the sacrifice of himself. Just as people are destined to die once, and after that to face judgment, so Christ was sacrificed once to take away the sins of many; and he will appear a second time, not to bear sin, but to bring salvation to those who are waiting for him.* (Hebrews 9:23–28)

The writer returns to the type/antitype relationship between the items in the earthly tabernacle and the more perfect heavenly tabernacle. Just as it was necessary for the copies on earth to be cleansed with blood on the Day of Atonement, so the real things in heaven had to be cleansed with blood. But in Jesus we have "better sacrifices" (v. 23). Jesus' blood is sprinkled in a much better tabernacle because this sanctuary was not "made with human hands" (v. 24), and besides, it is not a mere copy of the true one in which Jesus ministers to us. It is always the case that in the Old Testament we have a physical foreshadow to a spiritual reality found in the new covenant.

How do we know for sure that the sacrifice of Christ is better—that it is far more powerful in creating forgiveness of sins? We are told about Jesus, "Nor did he enter heaven to offer himself again and again" (v. 25) as the high priest entered the earthly holy of holies repeatedly under the regulations of the first covenant. A process that must be repeated an infinite number of times to complete the job is infinitely weaker than a process that definitively completes the job the first time. And besides, we are reminded that the high priests in the order of Aaron brought blood that was not their own. The sacrifice of Christ cost him incalculably more than the sacrifice brought by the Jewish high priest on the Day of Atonement. What a sacrifice we have in Jesus our high priest!

To further bring home to us the efficacy of the sacrifice of Jesus, we are asked to consider what it would be like if the blood of Christ was as ineffective as the blood of bulls and goats: "Otherwise Christ would have had to suffer many times since the creation of the world" (v. 26). But we know that Jesus is "the Lamb who was slain from the creation of the world" (Revelation 13:8). It is ludicrous to consider the idea of Jesus having to be crucified repeatedly. Hopefully by now, those hearing this sermon read to them have gotten the idea of how great Jesus is.

Then the Hebrew writer explains himself one more time with an analogy. How many times do we die? All of us know the answer to that question. Our death is completely effective at ending our physical life. In the same way, Christ only had to die for our sins once to effectively, totally, once and for all take away the sins of those who put their faith in him. The Hebrew writer is not creating an argument against belief in reincarnation (although this verse could be used that way). He is using a common-sense analogy to bring home to us the fact that we can be sure of our forgiveness through the sacrificial death of Jesus. We die once and then we face judgment, but we who are in Christ can have great confidence on the day of judgment because of the sacrificial death of Jesus. Jesus came to the earth to save, not to judge (John 12:47), but when he comes again at the end of time he will act to judge, not to save.

Jesus died once as an effective atoning sacrifice for our sins, but he was raised from the dead, he ascended to heaven and he will come back a second time (v. 28). The fact of his return is not evidence that his sacrifice was not effective! When he comes back, it will have nothing to do with forgiving our sins. That has already been taken care of. His second coming will be the culmination of the salvation that we have already, but not yet. In the New Testament, salvation is presented both as an event that happens at a definite point in time and as a process of change over time, which began with our initial salvation. So, in Christ we are saved already, but not yet. Our final, everlasting salvation will occur when Jesus comes again. In Hebrews 9:11–10:18 salvation is treated principally as an event that happens at a certain point in time. As William Lane said, "The writer's primary concern in this section is with objective salvation."[10] In Hebrews 9 we are being reminded that we are definitively saved if we are in Christ. It is in the five admonition sections of Hebrews that we are told how to practically bring our final salvation to completion—that we learn how to "work out [our] salvation with fear and trembling" (Philippians 2:12). This is the meaning of the statement that "Christ was sacrificed once to take away the sins of many; and he will appear a second time, not to bear sin, but to bring salvation to those who are waiting for him." In Hebrews 10:19 we will begin another section of the book, in which we will learn how it is that we can be sure to remain faithful to the end as we wait eagerly for his return.

Summary: The Case for the Superiority of Jesus' High Priestly Sacrifice

Hebrews 10:1–18 is the completion of a fairly long section of the book on the superiority of Jesus' sacrifice for our sins. It is a recapitulation of the entire argument of chapters 8 and 9. This is why it is logical that those who created chapter divisions began a new chapter after Hebrews 9:28. A good rule for a preacher is this: tell them what you are going to tell them, then tell them, then tell them what you told them. The last is what the Hebrew writer is doing for us in the first part of chapter ten. Remember as we study this section that the letter is addressed to Jewish Christians who have been sorely tempted to return to the comfort of Jewish ritual in order to escape the rigors of the pilgrim life of a disciple of Jesus.

The law is only a shadow of the good things that are coming—not the realities themselves. For this reason it can never, by the same sacrifices repeated endlessly year after year, make perfect those who draw near to worship. Otherwise, would they not have stopped being offered? For the worshipers would have been cleansed once for all, and would no longer have felt guilty for their sins. But those sacrifices are an annual reminder of sins. It is impossible for the blood of bulls and goats to take away sins.

Therefore, when Christ came into the world, he said:

"Sacrifice and offering you did not desire,
    but a body you prepared for me;
with burnt offerings and sin offerings
    you were not pleased.
Then I said, 'Here I am—it is written about me in the scroll—
    I have come to do your will, my God.'"

First he said, "Sacrifices and offerings, burnt offerings and sin offerings you did not desire, nor were you pleased with them"—though they were offered in accordance with the law. Then he said, "Here I am, I have come to do your will." He sets aside the first to establish the second. And by that will, we have been made holy through the sacrifice of the body of Jesus Christ once for all.

Day after day every priest stands and performs his religious duties; again and again he offers the same sacrifices, which can never take away sins. (Hebrews 10:1–11)

The writer of Hebrews opens his summary by reminding us of what he already told us, which is that the new covenant, established by the sacrifice of Jesus, is far superior to the old because it is the real thing. The law of Moses is only a shadow, a dim copy of that which it anticipates. Shadows have no power. They do not talk or eat or breathe. A shadow cannot really do anything. All it can "do" is give us a hint about the real thing of which it is a mere phantom. The Hebraic Christians to whom the letter is addressed were weary in their faith and fearful of new persecutions, which appeared to be coming on them. They were tempted to turn to reliance on Jewish forms of worship. But the covenant that was old and fading and about to completely disappear was ineffective. Even when it was in effect, its impact in creating real righteousness was limited. Now that Christ has come, fulfilling the law, the effectiveness of the first covenant at removing sins has dropped to zero. To turn to relying on the law would be a disastrous mistake.

The blessings we already have in Christ are real. The Greek word translated "realities" here is *eikon*, which means a realistic portrait or, in modern terms, a photograph. When we see Christ, we see as much of God as it is possible to see while still in a body. If we saw more we would be toast. He makes God known (John 1:18). He is the image of the invisible God (Colossians 1:15). This begs the question: why would those hearing this letter go back to a powerless imitation if they had access to the powerful reality? For the same reason you or I might do the exact same thing: The world wears us down. We fail to focus on Jesus. We become tired of making every effort. Our strength no longer comes from the true source, but from cheap imitations such as praises from the world and the pleasures of immediate gratification.

For this reason (that the law of Moses was merely a dim copy), it can never do for us what we desperately need, which is to give us a clean conscience before ourselves, before our fellow human beings and, most importantly, before God. How do we know that these sacrifices lack power? Because they must be "repeated endlessly year after year." Imagine you wanted to pursue a particular career. You went to the governing body of the profession and were told, "No problem. Just complete the training program." "Okay" you reply. "How long is the training program?" The response: "Endless." You would not sign up for that training program! It would never accomplish the goal you wanted to sign up to achieve in the first place. Such a program would be powerless and ultimately useless.

By the way, the sacrifices prescribed in the first covenant do have power, but the power was found in what they did not do rather than in what they did do. The power of these sacrifices was not to save. They were powerful at causing us to realize that we need Christ desperately. For the Jews, the Levitical sacrifices were an annual reminder of how sinful they were. The way Paul put it, "The law was brought in so that the trespass might increase" (Romans 5:20). He also said that "through the commandment" sin became "utterly sinful" (Romans 7:13). The power of the law was to cause us to realize in a graphic way how utterly sinful we are and how desperately we need a savior. Through the sacrifices in the Mosaic system, the Jews (and we) are reminded that sin is a terrible thing and warrants terrible judgment. We need a true and lasting forgiveness. This is what we have in the better sacrifice of Jesus.

After making this point, the writer brings it home to us one more time: "It is impossible for the blood of bulls and goats to take away sins" (v. 4). This is his third time telling us this truth. Hopefully we are getting it by now. You will remember from a previous chapter that there are four impossible things in Hebrews. It is impossible:

1. **To be renewed to repentance once fallen away (Hebrews 6:4–6)**

2. **For God to lie (Hebrews 6:18)**

3. **For the blood of bulls and goats to remove sins (Hebrews 10:4)**

4. **To please God without faith (Hebrews 11:6)**

This is why God "sets aside the first [covenant] to establish the second" (v. 9). He takes it away because it was powerless.

We will continue with this passage, but let us stop for a moment to consider something we just learned. If, in Christ, we have been cleansed of our sins "once for all," then God is telling us that we should no longer feel guilty for our sins. All of us sin and all of us who are saved feel guilty at times. However, we need to remind ourselves that in Christ we have been declared not guilty. We do not want to make you feel guilty that you feel guilty, but all of us need to be reminded at times that in God's eyes we are truly no longer held accountable. We are reconciled. Our sins are atoned for. Let us remind ourselves of this objective reality. Let us dwell on this startling fact and allow it sink in to our very souls so that we can receive the beautiful comfort that God intends for us.

Our own personal sacrifice does not bring about our salvation. This is found only in the all-sufficient sacrifice of Jesus. The writer of Hebrews brings this point home to us by quoting from Psalm 40:6–8. What does God want from us? He wants our humble submission and obedience to him, not our religious observances. Our preacher reads from Psalm 40:6, "Sacrifice and offering you did not desire," and then he repeats it for emphasis in verse 8, adding that God was not "pleased with them" (i.e., the sacrifices and offerings). Now, wait a minute; I am confused here. Didn't he command the Jews to make such burnt offerings and sin offerings? Yes, he did. Yes, they were "offered in accordance with the law" (v. 8). But that is not the point. Our sacrifices are to be offered, not in order to be saved, but as a free response of love from those who have already been saved. As Paul put it, "The only thing that counts is faith expressing itself through love" (Galatians 5:6). Do we get it? Our religious acts do absolutely zero to bring about our salvation, just as verse 11 tells us that "day after day every priest stands and performs his religious duties; again and again he offers the same sacrifices, which can never take away sins."

It is not that God does not want our sacrifices. He is delighted when we make personal sacrifices; they are a pleasing aroma to him (Leviticus 1:9, 2:2, 3:5, 8:28). He loves it. Our deeds, motivated by his grace, make his day. But we humans are constantly tempted to feel that our relationship with God and his love for us are dependent on these sacrifices. When we buy into this lie, we are sent on a guilt-ridden downward spiral. Let us not fall for this satanic trick; let us instead find comfort in the love and acceptance that we receive through Jesus our high priest.

Jesus demonstrated for us in the clearest possible way what God does want from us, which is a heart of obedience: "To obey is better than to sacrifice" (1 Samuel 15:22). "You did not delight in sacrifice, or I would bring it.... My sacrifice, O God, is a broken spirit; a broken and contrite heart you, God, will not despise" (Psalm 51:16–17). "For I desire mercy, not sacrifice, and acknowledgement of God rather than burnt offerings" (Hosea 6:6). Psalm 40:7–8, quoted in Hebrews 10:7, is a wonderful passage telling us what God really wants from us, but it is also a messianic prophecy: "Then I said, 'Here I am—it is written about me in the scroll—I have come to do your will, my God." In the Garden of Gethsemane, Jesus said, "My Father, if it is possible, may this cup be taken from me. Yet not as I will, but as you will." Jesus showed us the way of obedience. In his case, the obedience was perfect. In our case, we will never be perfect in our obedience, but what God wants from us is a heart of obedience. Our sincere desire to do his will, rather than perfection, is sufficient. Then Jesus' blood gets in there and transforms our imperfect but sincere desire to obey into perfection. This is a great encouragement!

When Jesus says, "a body you prepared for me," what he means is that the Father gave him a life in a physical body in which he could obey and serve the Father perfectly. Through the incarnation of the Son, we were shown that obedience from the heart is the only acceptable sacrifice to God. Let us remember that there was no sacrifice in the law of Moses to take care of willful sin. In other words, there was no sacrifice for willful disobedience. That is why we needed a more perfect sacrifice than that of bulls and goats. A heifer or a sheep cannot give willing obedience to God, because they do not have free will to bring into submission to God. Jesus was a willing sacrifice, and therefore he was a much greater one. The bull does not say, "Here I am," but Jesus did. For the rest of us, death ends our physical life, but for Jesus his death completed his life, because he gave it willingly in obedience to God. Therefore, "we have been made holy through the sacrifice of the body of Jesus Christ once for all" (v. 10). This is a beautiful thing.

Let us make the application to ourselves. If we want to make personal sacrifices to serve God, that is great. However, we should remember to do it in obedience to what God has told us to do and not to do. We should not go out and do our own thing, making the mistake of Saul in 1 Samuel 15, who disobeyed while supposedly "sacrificing." It is not wrong or bad to do the right thing because we "are supposed to." Sometimes that is the best we can offer, but it is always much better to give from a free and open heart that wants to serve, "not reluctantly or under compulsion" (2 Corinthians 9:7). This is the kind of sacrifice God wants from us, and it is the kind that will bring blessings on ourselves personally and on the Church.

Let us complete the thought in this section by contemplating Hebrews 10:11–18:

Day after day every priest stands and performs his religious duties; again and again he offers the same sacrifices, which can never take away sins. But when this priest had offered for all time one sacrifice for sins, he sat down at the right hand of God, and since that time he waits for his enemies to be made his footstool. For by one sacrifice he has made perfect forever those who are being made holy.

The Holy Spirit also testifies to us about this. First he says:
"This is the covenant I will make with them
after that time, says the Lord.
I will put my laws in their hearts,
and I will write them on their minds."

Then he adds:

"Their sins and lawless acts
I will remember no more."

And where these have been forgiven, sacrifice for sin is no longer necessary.

The writer of Hebrews makes a subtle shift here from talking about the Day of Atonement ("year after year" in verse 1) to the more mundane daily sacrifices that were a part of Judaism as prescribed in Leviticus ("day after day" in verse 11). What the sacrifices on the Day of Atonement did not accomplish, the daily routine of sacrifice in the temple or tabernacle also did not achieve. They did not bring about a true removal of guilt.

Another indicator of the weakness of the Levitical priesthood is that the priests descended from Aaron were allowed only to stand when they performed their religious duties in the tabernacle (v. 11). Mere servants stand when in the presence of their master, whereas we already know that Jesus is seated at the right hand of God in the heavenly sanctuary (Hebrews 1:13). This is because Jesus is both a servant/priest and a king. Not only is Jesus, as God, seated in the heavenly realms, but his enemies will be made a mere footstool before him. The purpose of a footstool is to be stepped on. Here the writer is referencing Psalm 110:1. This is the psalm about the priesthood of Melchizedek that is used repeatedly throughout Hebrews.

In 10:14 we have a beautiful summary of the stunning sacrifice of Jesus that makes us holy. It:

1. Is one sacrifice, and therefore no other is needed
2. Makes us perfect, and therefore is complete and finished, once for all time
3. Lasts forever, so that we already possess eternity, even in this life

Therefore, our author concludes by quoting one more time from Jeremiah 31:33–34, reminding us that we have a new and better covenant. His conclusion is this: where our sins have already been forgiven, the Old Testament sacrifices are no longer needed. So, let us move on to better things. We can summarize Hebrews 9:11–10:18 in this way: Jesus' death is the real thing, his blood is the real thing, the forgiveness he offers is the real thing, and the place where he offers it to serve us as a mediator is the real thing. It is time for our fourth admonition.

End Notes _____

9. https://www.chabad.org/library/article_cdo/aid/3613245/jewish/For-Real-How-Rare-Is-a-Red-Heifer.htm

10. William L. Lane, Hebrews 9–13, *Word Biblical Commentary vol. 47b* (Nashville, TN: Thomas Nelson, 1991), 251.

Chapter 14

Exhortation #4: Draw Near to God; Do Not Shrink Back
Hebrews 10:19–39

The preacher of Hebrews has now completed his argument about the vast superiority of Jesus Christ and of the covenant established in his blood. He will now turn almost exclusively to exhortation based on our conviction of the greatness of our Savior (although he will sprinkle in a few comments about the greatness of Jesus—he cannot help it!). We are calling Hebrews 10:19–39 exhortation #4, but it really is a series of exhortations. Before going into these, let us remember briefly the ways in which Jesus is greater than Moses and the covenant established through him.

1. Jesus is greater than the prophets (1:1–3).

2. Jesus is greater than the angels (1:4–1:14, 2:5–9).

3. Jesus is greater than Moses (3:1–6).

4. Jesus is greater than Joshua (4:8).

5. Jesus is greater than the high priest (4:14–5:10).

6. Jesus is greater than Abraham (6:13–20a, 7:4–5).

7. Jesus is greater than the priesthoods of Aaron and Melchizedek (6:20b–7:28).

8. Jesus' covenant is greater than the covenant of Moses (8:1–13).

9. Jesus dwells in a greater, heavenly tabernacle (9:1–11).

10. Jesus offers a greater sacrifice (9:12–10:18).

Actually, let us do more than remember the list of ways in which the priesthood of Jesus is superior. Let us take some time right now to stop reading. Let us take a break and spend some time meditating on how incredibly amazing it is that in Christ we have a high priest who removes our guilt and who opens the way for us—giving us full access to the very sanctuary of God...

We are about to consider a list of exhortations that, if we will accept them, will assure our salvation until the coming of Christ. If there ever was a set of exhortations we would do well to listen to, it is the ones in Hebrews 10–12. But we must remember that the key to putting these admonitions into effect and to completing our Christian journey is to consider Jesus, the pioneer and perfecter of our faith.

The word exhortation (Greek: *paraklesis*) can have a connotation of a strong admonition: if you are not doing this, you had better get started now! It can also have a connotation of pure encouragement and comfort. Such is the case with the first of our series of exhortations, in Hebrews 10:19–22:

> *Therefore, brothers and sisters, since we have confidence to enter the Most Holy Place by the blood of Jesus, by a new and living way opened for us through the curtain, that is, his body, and since we have a great priest over the house of God, let us draw near to God with a sincere heart and with the full assurance that faith brings, having our hearts sprinkled to cleanse us from a guilty conscience and having our bodies washed with pure water.*

It would be hard to think of any passage in all of Scripture more encouraging than this marvelous exhortation. It begins with "therefore." Whenever we see a "therefore" in the Bible, we should ask ourselves what it refers to. Generally it refers to the thing just said. Here we are being told that in view of what was just said, we should do something. What was just said is that we have a sacrifice in Christ that is once for all and that clears the way for us to have free access to the perfect, heavenly sanctuary.

In view of this amazing fact, what should we do? We should take full advantage of the opportunity afforded to us through the blood of Christ. We should take every opportunity to walk boldly into the presence of the God who created the entire universe and gave us life. We should lay our requests before God with boldness and with full confidence that he will stop what he is doing, get down on his knee and listen intently to what we have to say. Not only that, but because we have the Holy Spirit in us, he will even hear what is in our minds and hearts that our mere words can never express (Romans 8:26–27). He will hear us with an intimacy beyond that of any human, as he knows our deepest thoughts and feelings.

To make this even more wonderful, our Father will not judge us for the ugly thoughts that are still buried in there. We can have full assurance of this! By faith we understand that our hearts have been sprinkled with the cleansing power of the blood of Jesus and our consciences have been scrubbed perfectly clean of all guilt in the pure waters of baptism. No baptism, no washing (Acts 22:16) and therefore no access, but we have been washed, so we have access. We need not hide our deepest, darkest secrets in the presence of God as we pray, because he has already declared us not guilty. Even our closest friends and family might possibly judge us, but the Father will not. We have been granted full immunity. In the presence of God, perfect love drives out all fear (1 John 4:18).

What would you pay for such access? Well, guess what, the price is already paid! Our high priest Jesus has blazed the trail into the real holy of holies. He is already in there speaking for us. "This is my sister. I can vouch for her. She is perfect and without sin. Father, listen to her, show compassion to her, and answer her prayers if they agree with your will." What an advocate we have. We have a defense lawyer who never loses a case.

So, what is stopping you? Is there a small part of you that simply does not believe you are without guilt in God's presence? Then you ought to read and study Hebrews chapter 11. Even if your faith has not yet brought the "full assurance" mentioned above, walk into God's presence anyway. Maybe your level of boldness in the presence of God is not quite there yet. Then enter with all the confidence you can muster and let Jesus minister to you. We need to pray, and in prayer, we need to grasp how stupendous it is that we have access to the presence of our Father in heaven. Think about it. Take some time to contemplate this staggering fact. We have:

1. **Confidence**
2. **Full assurance**
3. **Consciences cleansed of all guilt**

How did we gain this access? Through "a new and living way opened for us through the curtain, that is, his body." There are two possible interpretations of this statement about our means of access to the holy of holies:

1. The body of Jesus is the means by which we are able to pass through the curtain/veil and gain access to the real inner sanctuary.

Or

2. We gain access to the real inner sanctuary through his body, which is, figuratively, the curtain that prevented our full access to the Father under the first covenant.

If the first statement is correct, then what God means here is that the body of Jesus, or more precisely his willing offering of his body as a sacrifice, has given us the means of full access to the throne of God. This is the more "obvious" meaning of the text. Even if it is not the one intended by the writer of Hebrews, it is still true!

The second interpretation is the less obvious one, but it is the one preferred by most scholars. If you look at the punctuation in most translations, you can see that this is what translators intend: "through the curtain [comma] that is [comma] his body." In other words, as long as Jesus was still in his physical body here on the earth, the way to full and unfettered access to the inner sanctuary in heaven was still not yet open. It was when he gave up his body on the cross that the way was opened. In that sense, his body, which he still occupied at that time, was the curtain. It was the thing that separated us from God. His physical death, like the veil, stood between Jesus and his fully realized relationship with God in his heavenly sanctuary.

Despite the opinion of the scholars, we prefer the first interpretation, but in any case, the result is the same: we have access, and we can enter confidently into the presence of God. Let us focus on this.

Our author tells us that this means of access is "new and living" (v. 20). It is new, both in the sense that it was only granted quite recently and in the sense that it is a totally new kind of access. This means of admission to the throne of God was only about thirty years old when Hebrews was written, and nothing like it had ever been seen before. It is a living way, a continual and lifegiving means of access to God.

Our author uses the phrase "let us" as his manner of expressing exhortation. He has a few more of these "let us" admonitions for us:

> Let us hold unswervingly to the hope we profess, for he who promised is faithful. And let us consider how we may spur one another on toward love and good deeds, not giving up meeting together, as some are in the habit of doing, but encouraging one another—and all the more as you see the Day approaching. (Hebrews 10:23–25)

Our principle motivation for holding unswervingly to the hope we profess will come from looking at Christ. Our hope is the anchor behind the veil—Jesus Christ. This is the hope that will keep us on course. It will keep us from swerving off the narrow road that leads to life. We cannot allow Satan to steal that hope from us.

However, our preacher is a shepherd who is well aware that at times we need encouragement from a more visible source of motivation. We need one another to get to heaven. Christianity is lived out in a local fellowship of believers, in submission to godly leaders (Hebrews 13:17). Solitary Christianity is an oxymoron. All of the members of the Church, being members of a family, have both privileges and responsibilities that come with being part of a family. We are our brother's and sister's keepers—we have a responsibility to spur one another on, to hang out with one another and to encourage one another. There are five "let us" admonitions is this section. These exhortations are to exercise faith, hope and love.

- **Faith: Let us draw near with full assurance (v. 22)**
- **Hope: Let us hold unswervingly to the hope we profess (v. 23)**
- **Love: Let us be concerned about one another and motivate one another (v. 24)**
- **Let us continue to meet together (v. 25)**
- **Let us encourage one another (v. 25)**

Who have you "spurred on" toward love and good deeds this week? This spurring on may involve loving confrontation: "As iron sharpens iron, so one person sharpens another" (Proverbs 27:17). If we are all to get to heaven, we will have to speak the truth in love to one another (Ephesians 4:15). Such truth-speaking is often not enjoyable, but love requires that we do it. The enduring strength of our relationship with God depends on others doing this for us at times. Conversely, the ultimate salvation of our Christian friends may depend on us spurring them along in practicing their faith as well.

Hopefully, you rarely if ever miss meetings of your local church. If you do so habitually, you are stealing from the hope and assurance both of yourself and of your brothers and sisters. Sometimes (but hopefully rarely) part of Christianity is just showing up. When you miss family meetings, you can negatively impact the level of encouragement and faith of your family members. If we make a habit of missing the assemblies of God's Church, we may end up in a place where Hebrews 10:26–31 applies to us. Let us humbly accept this admonishment and put it into practice. Don't miss church!

Hopefully, we will do a lot more than just show up. Jesus said that "it is more blessed to give than to receive" (Acts 20:35). We should not go to church principally to get our own needs met, but to encourage the faith of others. If all the members of the family do their part, guess what! You will be greatly encouraged as well. William Barclay said, "No man ever saved his soul who devoted his whole time and energy to saving it; but many a man has saved his soul by being so concerned for others that he forgot that he himself had a soul to save."[11] Selfish Christianity is a contradiction in terms.

Having given us some very practical admonitions to love one another and therefore to help one another continue in our faith, God turns us to the most solemn warning in Hebrews. Let us read this section for a second time:

> If we deliberately keep on sinning after we have received the knowledge of the truth, no sacrifice for sins is left, but only a fearful expectation of judgment and of raging fire that will consume the enemies of God. Anyone who rejected the law of Moses died without mercy on the testimony of two or three witnesses. How much more severely do you think someone deserves to be punished who has trampled the Son of God underfoot, who has treated as an unholy thing the blood of the covenant that sanctified them, and who has insulted the Spirit of grace? For we know him who said, "It is mine to avenge; I will repay," and again, "The Lord will judge his people." It is a dreadful thing to fall into the hands of the living God. (Hebrews 10:26–31)

If, as Christians, we "ignore so great a salvation," if we do not make every effort, if we do not move on to maturity, if we fail to regularly enter confidently into the presence of God, if we do not give and receive admonition from one another, if we make a habit of missing church meetings, and if we fail to offer and accept encouragement from one another, then it is very likely that we will find ourselves in a state of deliberate and continual sin. If this persists over time, then we will find ourselves separated from the God who saved us. This is truly a terrifying prospect, yet it certainly can happen. One of the motivations for the writing of Hebrews was that this was becoming a real possibility for the hearers of the book. The overall tenor of Hebrews is positive. The author is "convinced of better things" in our case (Hebrews 6:9), and he believes that "we do not belong to those who shrink back and are destroyed" (Hebrews 10:39). But as a shepherd of God's people and as a watchman of Israel (Ezekiel 3:16–21), it is his solemn duty to warn us about the horror of apostasy from the faith.

We already analyzed this section of the sermon when we discussed the possibility of falling away in the context of Hebrews 6:4–8. However, a few additional comments are called for here in light of our study of Hebrews 7:1–10:18. Given the greater high priesthood, the better covenant, our access to the true tabernacle, and the perfect sacrifice we have in Jesus, how great a crime against God it would be if we were to turn our backs on what he has given us. The writer of Hebrews reasons with us rationally concerning a very emotional topic. Logically, if we reject a greater gift than what the Jews had under the old covenant, then the negative consequences of that rejection would be much greater than those that Israel experienced. The natural outcome of rejecting Christ, who is over God's house, is far worse than that of rejecting Moses, who was merely the greatest in God's house. "How much more severely do you think someone deserves to be punished who has trampled the Son of God underfoot, who has treated as an unholy thing the blood of the covenant that sanctified them, and who has insulted the Spirit of grace?" This is inescapable logic. However, it is the emotional impact of the horror of sin and the terrifying consequences of apostasy which God wants us to take into our hearts and minds.

The Hebrew writer quotes from Deuteronomy 32:35. If we treat as an unholy thing that which made us holy—the blood of Jesus—and if we insult the Holy Spirit, whom he caused to live in us as God dwells in his temple, then God solemnly warns us, "It is mine to avenge: I will repay" and "The Lord will judge his people." Let us decide right now that we will do anything possible to avoid this terrible fate. Let us come confidently into the presence of God, let us cling tenaciously to the hope we have, and let us see to it in love that our brothers and sisters do so as well. If we do, then we do not need to live in fear. If we fear God properly, then we do not need to live in a state of perpetual dread of him. It is the intention of God that we live in a sense of confidence and hope.

Having received this most grave of warnings, we come to a further, more encouraging exhortation:

> Remember those earlier days after you had received the light, when you endured in a great conflict full of suffering. Sometimes you were publicly exposed to insult and persecution; at other times you stood side by side with those who were so treated. You suffered along with those in prison and joyfully accepted the confiscation of your property, because you knew that you yourselves had better and lasting possessions. So do not throw away your confidence; it will be richly rewarded.
>
> You need to persevere so that when you have done the will of God, you will receive what he has promised. For,
>
> > "In just a little while,
> > > he who is coming will come
> > > and will not delay."
>
> And,
>
> > "But my righteous one will live by faith.
> > > And I take no pleasure
> > > in the one who shrinks back."
>
> But we do not belong to those who shrink back and are destroyed, but to those who have faith and are saved. (Hebrews 10:32–39)

Do you remember the day you were baptized into Christ? You were incredibly encouraged by the new hope you had found. For the first time in your life, you had the prospect of living free of guilt. Sharing your faith with your friends was the most natural thing in the world. Insults from your coworkers or family members over your newfound faith were an encouragement to you that you were doing the right thing, not a reason to feel defeated.

But over time, the "reality" of life chipped away at your confidence in Christ. The outward cares and worries of life—the visible things—began to get more of your notice than the less visible but more important spiritual reality that you were forgiven of your sin and were impacting others for eternity. What you need is a call to persevere. The world can take away the physical things from you, but they cannot steal your salvation unless you let them. You have great victories behind you, and, if you will hold on to your faith, even greater victories lie before you. But even if you do not experience greater victories, you have everything that is truly important. You are saved. You have been declared not guilty by the only judge that matters. You have access through High Priest Jesus to the inner sanctuary.

If you are in need of this call to persevere, then you are in the same boat as the recipients of Hebrews. They had started the race well. God was very proud of their service to the saints. In their zeal for Jesus, they had accepted persecution and suffering for the name. Besides, they were well past the midpoint of the race. They were already qualified for the prize, and all they really had to do was keep on running the race. Final victory was all but assured. Yet some of them were in danger of quitting the race and losing everything they had lived for. What greater tragedy could there be?

These Christians had endured far more than most of us have experienced in our walk with God. They had suffered confiscation of their property and been fired up about the privilege of receiving such ill treatment for the sake of Christ. This was no minor persecution! The fact that they could accept such treatment for the sake of Christ as a great blessing is an upward call to all of us. What had changed for these believers who had endured so much for their Lord? The answer is that over time, the things of the world had caused them to lose sight of the prize. They were looking back to Egypt and failing to look forward to their eternal rest in the promised land. Why had they been able to endure as younger disciples what they could no longer accept as older Christians? Because in earlier times they were more keenly aware that they themselves "had better and lasting possessions."

Some of us have allowed the world to beat us up spiritually. We have lost sight of those better and lasting possessions. We must listen to this exhortation: "You need to persevere so that when you have done the will of God, you will receive what he has promised" (v. 36). Don't even think about throwing it all away! The finish line is in sight. Can you see it? "In just a little while, he who is coming will come and will not delay." Shrinking back is not an option! (v. 37). What are you thinking?

I (John) described my climb up Mount Whitney in a previous chapter. I will never forget reaching the 13,800-foot level. I was completely exhausted, jetlagged, suffering from a severe cold and barely able to put one foot in front of the other. But then I came around a bend in the trail, and the final ascent to the summit came into view. There was NO WAY that I was going to turn around at that point. Just imagining getting so close and not making the top was something I could not accept. I needed to persevere. In just a little while I would achieve my goal. I was not about to shrink back. Well, guess what, I made it and I am so glad I was able to fix my eyes on the goal, or I probably would have turned back.

This is a pretty good analogy for what God is trying to tell us in Hebrews 10, but there are two differences. First, the stakes in our Christian journey are infinitely greater than reaching the top of a mountain. We are talking about our eternal destiny. "Therefore we do not lose heart.... For our light and momentary troubles are achieving for us an eternal glory that far outweighs them all. So we fix our eyes not on what is seen, but on what is unseen, since what is seen in temporary, but what is unseen is eternal" (2 Corinthians 4:16–18). Infinity divided by any finite number produces the mathematical result of infinity. There is no viable alternative. We must persevere. There is way too much at stake.

There is a second difference between the Mount Whitney example and our Christian walk. There was something about actually seeing the peak that provided great motivation to keep going. Our goal—heaven—is not something we can see with our physical vision. Only through the eyes of faith can we see "the prize for which God has called [us] heavenward in Christ Jesus" (Philippians 3:14). We need to learn to see through faithful eyes. But that is exactly what we will be called to do in Hebrews 11.

Let us end our study of Hebrews 10 with a great encouragement from our biggest fan—God. "But we do not belong to those who shrink back and are destroyed, but to those who have faith and are saved." Let us hold on and stay in the race. We will be richly rewarded when we reach the peak.

End Notes _____

11. William Barclay, *The Letter to the Hebrews* (Philadelphia: Westminster Press, 1976), 121.

____ Chapter 15 ____

Exhortation #5: Live by Faith
Hebrews 11:1–40

We have now reached the key moment in our sermon. This section is what the writer had in mind from the beginning. It is here that he makes the central appeal of Hebrews. What is the one thing that, if we get it, we get the entire book? What is the one exhortation that summarizes all the others and which, if we will put it into practice, will surely get us to the prize? It is the call for us to live by faith. We are excited—how about you? Let's get started.

> *Now faith is confidence in what we hope for and assurance about what we do not see. This is what the ancients were commended for.*
> *By faith we understand that the universe was formed at God's command, so that what is seen was not made out of what is visible.* (Hebrews 11:1–3)

What is faith? Is it believing the facts of the Bible? Is it a willingness to obey what God commands? Is it fully trusting God's providence in our lives? Yes, it is all those things, but in Hebrews 11 God defines faith in the way that is relevant to his goal, which is to get us across the finish line and bring us into our eternal rest. Faith is confidently holding on to the hope of our salvation, a constant assurance that God will do what he said he will do. Faith involves the future. It also involves the present, but whether the present or the future, our faith is in things which cannot be seen.

Think about it. Every single thing that is important is invisible. Everything that is visible or that can be touched or tasted or smelled is relatively unimportant. Go ahead. Make a list of the things you truly value. If you are a Christian, then probably all or nearly all of them are invisible. On a heart level, what are you putting your faith in?

The Hebrew writer illustrates the relative importance of invisible things in verse 2 by reminding us that the visible universe was created by and invisible God. If what is visible was created by one who is invisible, then surely the invisible is greater in every way than the visible.

I (John) am a Christian apologist. This does not mean that I go around apologizing for being a Christian. It means that one of my roles is presenting evidence that supports the conclusion that the Bible is the inspired word of God and that Jesus is the way to eternal life. Some say that trying to prove the Bible is pretty much a waste of time because evidence is something we can see, but faith involves things we cannot see. It is the things we cannot "see", the things that require faith, which actually matter. People who say this have a point. If we can see something, believing in it is not faith. However, their conclusion that we do not need evidence is not a valid point. People who say this are correct to this extent: if our "faith" in God is based only on evidence, then it is truly a shallow faith and will not allow us to do much for God. Instead, the things that have been proved to us by evidence should cause us to step out even further into areas that require faith. The more evidence we have, the more we should rely on God in ways about which we have no evidence. We do need to live by our faith.

Faith requires that we deny our senses. Our senses tell us one thing, and faith tells us something quite different. My senses tell me that I am getting older, my body is decaying and it is all downhill from here. Faith tells me that "our light and momentary troubles are achieving for us an eternal glory that far outweighs them all" (2 Corinthians 4:17). Why? "For we live by faith, not by sight" (2 Corinthians 5:7). The Bible tells us that God is in control. If we watch the news, does it appear that God is in control? Not really! Faith requires that we not let our minds be ruled by what we can see. The world chases after observable things. We are different. The world thinks we are out of our mind, and from their point of view, they are right, since the things we seek are not evident to them.

Success is one example of something you can "see." In that sense, success is the enemy of real biblical faith. Is your feeling of confidence that God is with you and that things are right with the world based on whether or not you are succeeding? All of us want "success" in our spiritual lives, whether it be seeing others won to Christ, growth in our own spiritual walk, our children experiencing fulfillment or even people respecting us for our accomplishments. God understands this, and he wants us to have these things. However, sometimes he will take such things away from us for a time because "God disciplines us for our good" (Hebrews 12:10). Is your "faith" reliant on visible success? If so, then it is placed in something seen and if, for whatever reason, God allows you to go through an extended period without outward achievement, you are in for a really big fall.

"This is what the ancients were commended for." What is the point being made here? We will see repeated many times throughout this chapter that these heroes of faith believed in things that they did not see, even though they had so much less to base that faith on than we have. None of them had the New Testament. They had great promises from God, but we have the promises fulfilled in Jesus Christ. To them the Messiah was a vague idea. Some of them had the shadow available to them, but we have the reality in our hands. Surely, then, we can walk by faith in God. Peter reminded his hearers that because he and the other apostles beheld Jesus' ministry firsthand, "we have the prophetic word strongly confirmed" (2 Peter 1:19 HCSB).

What do all of these men and women of faith in the Old Testament have in common? They looked at the things that the world had to offer—the things that can be seen—and considered them worthless compared to having a relationship with God. They decided instead to trust fully in an unseen God to take care of them. They became strangers in this world but became honored citizens in the kingdom of God. Are you willing to live out this kind of life?

This is the attitude Paul took. By the religious standards of his day, he was a religious superstar. He was headed for a great career as a Pharisee.

> *If someone else thinks they have reasons to put confidence in the flesh, I have more: circumcised on the eighth day, of the people of Israel, of the tribe of Benjamin, a Hebrew of Hebrews; in regard to the law, a Pharisee; as for zeal, persecuting the church; as for righteousness based on the law, faultless.* (Philippians 3:4–6)

Paul had quite a pedigree. But he saw these outward accomplishments as part of the flesh, even though they were religious things. Here is what he said with regard to outward, visible, religious accomplishment: "What is more, I consider everything a loss because of the surpassing worth of knowing Christ Jesus my Lord" (Philippians 3:8). He considered his outward accomplishments as of no value, saying he considered these things garbage, that he might gain Christ. To him they were worth less than zero. On the cosmic balance-sheet they added up to a negative number. They were a loss in comparison to the invisible relationship we have with God through our high priest Jesus.

Paul and Solomon are opposite sides of the same coin. Both had everything. Solomon had everything that the world has to offer. Paul had everything that religion has to offer. If fulfillment could be achieved through gaining the "stuff" of the world, then Solomon would know, because he had it all. His take on the question: "Meaningless." If our inner needs could be met through religious accomplishment, then Paul would know. His take on the question: he considered it all a loss. What about you? What things grab your attention? What are you putting your hope in?

Let me share a story of a good friend who chose not to look at the visible things of this world. It comes from my friend Quoc Hung. He and his wife were leading a church in Ho Chi Minh City (formerly Saigon) and planned on planting a church in Hanoi, Vietnam. They were used to receiving a lot of persecution. Three times they have been kicked out of their meeting place and their home. They cannot have visitors come to their meetings for fear of the church being exposed. On the day they were sending out the mission team to Hanoi, the father of a young Christian burst into their apartment and beat Quoc Hung with a broomstick right in front of his wife, children and mother. The man was angered by his son's conversion. As for the visible signs, it was a bad idea to go and plant that church in Hanoi. All the things that can be seen said, "No!" Nevertheless, just a few days later, with Quoc Hung still visibly bruised from the beating, they went to plant the church. On the very day of their arrival in Hanoi, a police officer knocked on their door. "Did you come here to plant a church?" What would you have said? "Are you the group that teaches you must be totally committed to be a true Christian?" To both questions, Quoc Hung, despite all outward appearance that this was a bad idea, said "Yes." The police officer then said, "I have been waiting for you for so long, and now you are here. Please teach me the Bible." He was the first baptism in the Hanoi church. Faith is belief in things unseen. Quoc Hung and his wife believe this basic truth of Christianity, and they put it into practice.

In the story we read in Daniel chapter 3, what did Shadrach, Meshach and Abednego see? They saw the most powerful man in the world up on the stage, a fiery furnace and tens of thousands of people bowing down to a pagan statue. Based on visible things, it did not look like a good idea to stand up for God, but these teenagers did exactly that. Furious with rage, Nebuchadnezzar had them dragged before him. He pointed out the obvious, based on outward appearance, which is that his god Bel was more powerful than Yahweh. How could he be so sure? The items from the Jewish temple were sitting in his treasury. He gave these intrepid teenagers one more chance to change their minds. To the most powerful man on earth at that time, who had the power of life or instant death over them, they said in response:

"King Nebuchadnezzar, we do not need to defend ourselves before you in this matter. If we are thrown into the blazing furnace, the God we serve is able to deliver us from it, and he will deliver us from Your Majesty's hand. But even if he does not, we want you to know, Your Majesty, that we will not serve your gods or worship the image of gold you have set up." (Daniel 3:16–18)

Where did such supernatural courage come from? It came from faith in the unseen. Did they have some sort of assurance that they would survive the flames? Probably not. The deliverance they were so sure of was not visible to them. It was deliverance in that the faithful will be with God for eternity. One thing we can say for sure is that those of us who have the New Testament have far more reason for assurance than these three young men did. They chose to ignore what is seen, and God made them an example to us of what it means to walk by faith. By faith, they walked right up to that fiery furnace, and God did indeed deliver them. But even if he had not physically rescued them, the message of the story would be the same, would it not?

Starting in verse 4 our writer proceeds to present to us the hall of fame of the faithful. In every case, these men and women believed, not because of what they could see, but in spite of what was seen.

By faith Abel brought God a better offering than Cain did. By faith he was commended as righteous, when God spoke well of his offerings. And by faith Abel still speaks, even though he is dead. (Hebrews 11:4)

We do not know a lot about Abel. We are not even sure why his offering was so much more faithful than that of Cain. But one thing we do know about him: because of his faithful obedience, he is commended to us as righteous. And we are still talking about him today. What do you want people to say about you after you die? Wouldn't it be great if they said about you, "She was one of the most faithful women I have ever known." What better thing could we be commended for? Because of Abel's faith, he "still speaks, even though he is dead." This could be you.

Then, of course, there is Enoch. Again, we do not know a lot about him, but one thing we know for sure is that he walked by faith.

> By faith Enoch was taken from this life, so that he did not experience death: "He could not be found, because God had taken him away." For before he was taken, he was commended as one who pleased God. And without faith it is impossible to please God, because anyone who comes to him must believe that he exists and that he rewards those who earnestly seek him. (Hebrews 11:5–6)

Enoch's walk was so faithful that God decided to open a stairway directly to heaven for him. He completely skipped the normal process of dying. What does God want from you and from me? What will help to assure us of our salvation? We need to believe that God exists, even though we cannot see him. This kind of faith is relatively easy to attain. If we look at the physical world, never mind the unseen spiritual world, "God's invisible qualities—his eternal power and divine nature—have been clearly seen, being understood from what has been made known, so that people are without excuse" (Romans 1:20). Notice Paul's mention of God's "invisible" qualities.

It is not hard to believe that God exists, but the second requirement is much more challenging. Do you truly believe, in the deepest part of your being, that God will reward you if you earnestly seek him and trust in him alone? Do you believe that if you look away from your own accomplishments and gifts, that if you put zero reliance on your own educational achievements and put aside your own plans, trusting fully and completely in God for the direction of your life, that he will take care of you? Do you believe that his plans for you are better than your own? Can you let go completely of the things of the world? Can you put your full weight of faith in the invisible kingdom of God? If so, then you are like Enoch, and you will also be welcomed into the eternal kingdom as a hero of the faith.

You know that our storyteller has been waiting eagerly to share the account of the faith of Noah. Here we truly have a man who believed in things that are not seen.

> *By faith Noah, when warned about things not yet seen, in holy fear built an ark to save his family. By faith he condemned*

*the world and became heir of the righteousness that is in
keeping with faith.* (Hebrews 11:7)

Consider the faith of Noah: to say that God warned him about things
not yet seen is an understatement! Imagine that we were there, listening in
on the conversation:

"Noah!"
"Yes, Lord."
"I want you to build an ark."
"What's an ark? I have never seen one of those."
"It's a big boat—one that will save you from the water that is coming."
"What water?"
"I am sending a flood."
"What's a flood? I have never seen a flood."
"It is going to rain and rain and rain until the earth is covered with
water as far as the eye can see."
"OK, how big an ark do I need to build?"
"Three hundred cubits by fifty cubits by thirty cubits." (about 130 x 25
x 14 meters)
"Why such a big boat?"
"Because of the animals"
"What animals?"
"The ones I am going to send."
"When are they coming?"
"In a hundred years."

None of these things had ever been seen. Yet by faith Noah built that
ark, and by faith he saved his family from death. Imagine the conversation
with his wife! "Wife, guess what!" (To us she is known only as Noah's wife.)
"We are going to build an ark." "What's an ark?" "It's a really big boat."
You can imagine the conversation from there. We can see her asking, "Now,
which God told you to do this?" Noah's response, "The God you can't see."
We can imagine a similar conversation with the neighbors. "Noah, what
are you doing?" "I'm building an ark." "What's an ark?" They must have
thought he was crazy, and by the standards of the world they were right.
They must have laughed at him and talked all the time behind his back. Yet
by faith, Noah built the ark. When the door to the ark was shut and the rain

came down in torrents, no one was laughing at Noah, but for them it was too late. Consider this: If we trust in God in spite of what is seen, we can be a Noah for those in our lives.

Noah believed despite what was seen. As for visible "success," he preached for one hundred years,[12] but did not have a single convert. We are tempted to be discouraged when our faithful declaration of the gospel does not produce immediate results. Noah may not have seen great "success" in his life, but consider how many have come to God since his death. His faith has led to the salvation of many, although he never saw its fruit.

Our greatest example of one who walked by faith is Abraham. "He is the father of us all" (Romans 4:16) because of his faithful walk.

> By faith Abraham, when called to go to a place he would later receive as his inheritance, obeyed and went, even though he did not know where he was going. By faith he made his home in the promised land like a stranger in a foreign country; he lived in tents, as did Isaac and Jacob, who were heirs with him of the same promise. For he was looking forward to the city with foundations, whose architect and builder is God. And by faith even Sarah, who was past childbearing age, was enabled to bear children because she considered him faithful who had made the promise. And so from this one man, and he as good as dead, came descendants as numerous as the stars in the sky and as countless as the sand on the seashore. (Hebrews 11:8–12)

"Abraham believed God, and it was credited to him as righteousness" (Genesis 15:6; Romans 4:3). What did Abraham believe? He believed that when God makes a promise he fulfills it; and he was willing to act on that faith. He believed this, not because of what is seen, but in spite of visible evidence to the contrary. If we will believe in the unseen things of God, it will be credited to us as righteousness as well. But this is not an easy thing to do.

We can imagine a conversation somewhat like that with Noah:

"Abraham!"
"Yes, Lord."
"I want you to leave everything behind and go."
"Great, where am I going?"

"I am not going to tell you. Just start on your journey, then I will tell you where you're going."

"Can you give me a hint? Should I start out to the South, the North, the East or the West?"

"Just go."

"When will we come back?"

"Never."

Imagine the exchange when he came home. "Sarai, get packed. We're going on a trip." "Okay, great. Where are we going, and when are we coming back?" "I have no idea where we're going, and we are never coming back." This was probably not an easy sell. But by faith, Abram left Ur, even though he did not know where he was going.[13] And to be fair, Sarai deserves a lot of credit for her faith as well. We need to follow Abraham's and Sarah's faithful footsteps out of Ur ourselves. Actually, if you are a disciple of Jesus, you already have. You have already given up everything you have to follow him (Luke 14:33).

Abram had a comfortable living situation. He had wealth, a loving family, a solid reputation and every prospect of a happy, normal life in Ur. Yet by faith he began his Christian adventure. He spent the rest of his life living in tents, traveling from place to place. He lived in Canaan, which was a mere picture, a prefigure of the real promised land that God is holding out for us. The only part of the promise he actually received during his lifetime was a postage-stamp-sized piece of land in Canaan (Genesis 23:3–20). Are you ready for your own Christian adventure? We are tempted to ask God ahead of time where we are headed. But if we can see the place where we are going, there is little if any faith required for that journey. Are you prepared to set out on a faithful journey and let God determine the path? "Will he give me a spouse?" We do not know. "Will I be able to settle down in this career and in this city?" If we knew the answer, then that would not require faith.

Abram believed God's promises, even when they appeared to defy reason. Because of his faith, he received the name Abraham, and his wife became Sarah. Arguably, the three most faithful in all of Scripture are Noah, Abraham and Mary. Mary is an example of miraculous faith in spite of what is seen. The angel informed her that she would be with child, even though she was a virgin. This is not how pregnancy ordinarily is started. Outward appearances dictated that she would be put aside by Joseph, be refused marriage for life, live in abject poverty and be considered a sinner and an outcast until the day she died. Yet she said to the angel, "I am the Lord's servant, may your word to me be fulfilled." Now that is faith!

Abraham was in his nineties and Sarah in her eighties. When he was told by God that he would have a son, he probably felt he still had it in him, but when he looked at Sarah, things did not look so good in the baby-bearing department. She had been childless through her entire childbearing years, and menopause was forty years behind her. No one had ever given birth in their eighties, never mind a barren woman. Yet by faith both Abraham and Sarah believed, and Abraham became the father of many nations. This promise was fulfilled literally, as Abraham became the father of the Arabs, the Edomites and the Jews. It was also fulfilled figuratively, because Abraham has millions of spiritual children. As Paul said in Romans, he is the father of all who, by faith, leave their own Ur behind and put their entire trust, not in the things of the world, but in God. If you are a Christian, then you are one of Abraham's children.

We are going to skip Hebrews 11:13–17 temporarily so that we can finish the story of faithful Abraham.

> *By faith Abraham, when God tested him, offered Isaac as a sacrifice. He who had embraced the promises was about to sacrifice his one and only son, even though God had said to him, "It is through Isaac that your offspring will be reckoned." Abraham reasoned that God could even raise the dead, and so in a manner of speaking he did receive Isaac back from death.* (Hebrews 11:17–19)

This has to be the greatest single example of living by faith in the Scriptures, unless we consider Jesus' faithful journey to the cross. Just imagine the quandary that God's command to Abraham put him into. The way the early Christian leader Chrysostom put it, "The things of God seemed to fight against the things of God, and faith fought with faith, and the commandment fought with the promise." The promise was that Abraham would have a son and that many nations would come from that son. But then God asked Abraham to kill that same son. Was Abraham going to obey in faith, even if it would appear to nullify the promise? Amazingly, Abraham resolutely set out for Moriah the next day (Genesis 22:1–14). He was willing to kill his one and only son and heir on Mount Moriah.

This is the same mountain on which Jerusalem is built (2 Chronicles 3:1). Abraham willingly offered the promised son on the same mountain where God offered his one and only Son. Paul tells us in 1 Corinthians 15:4 that it was prophesied in the Old Testament that the Messiah would be raised on the third day. The prophecy is found right here in Genesis 22. From the time he set out for Moriah, to Abraham, Isaac was as good as dead. As the Hebrew writer tells us, figuratively Abraham received his son back from the dead—and it happened on the third day.

Notice what we are told here: "Abraham reasoned that God could even raise the dead." Some say that true faith requires that we stop thinking rationally and obey blindly. This is not what Abraham did. He had the promise from God that he would be the father of many nations through Isaac. Yet the command was to kill Isaac, which seemed to be in incontrovertible conflict with the promise. In what must have been a long and sleepless night, Abraham considered the promise and the command and came to the only reasonable conclusion as to how the promise could be fulfilled and he could at the same time faithfully obey the command of God. He put one and one together and got two, but his conclusion is one that none of us would have reached, unless our faith were marvelous indeed. The only way through this seemingly impossible paradox was this: Abraham told himself that God intended to raise Isaac from the dead after he killed him, as this was the only conceivable way the promise and the command could be justified. As far as we know, this came from Abraham's mind, not from any revelation. Abraham's faith was astounding, but it was also reasonable. The world will not see it as reasonable, but what is reasonable to a person of faith is not the same as to a person whose trust is based on the visible things of this world. Based on his reasoning, combined with his faith, Abraham left with Isaac for Mount Moriah.

We need to follow the steps of faith of Abraham out of Ur, and we need to follow his steps to Moriah. What is Mount Moriah, figuratively? It is the place where we trust God and allow him to take away from us the blessings he has given us. These are things we have received, even after beginning our faith journey. In his providence and his wisdom, God may take away from you your most precious possession—maybe it will be your career or your accomplishment, or maybe it will be your child, your spouse or even your own life. Will you trust him as Abraham did? "Abraham believed, and it was credited to him as righteousness." It was in response to this one enormous act of faith that God said to Abraham, "I swear by myself, declares the Lord, that because you have done this and have not withheld your son, your only son, I will surely bless you and make your descendants as numerous as the stars in the sky and as the sand on the seashore" (Genesis 22:16–17). God has a similar promise and oath for us.

The heart of the greatest exhortation in Hebrews is found in 11:13–17. It is here that the author summarizes for us what it means to live and to walk by faith.

> *All these people were still living by faith when they died. They did not receive the things promised; they only saw them and welcomed them from a distance, admitting that they were foreigners and strangers on earth. People who say such things show that they are looking for a country of their own. If they had been thinking of the country they had left, they would have had opportunity to return. Instead, they were longing for a better country—a heavenly one. Therefore God is not ashamed to be called their God, for he has prepared a city for them.* (Hebrews 11:13–17)

If you are reading this book, then presumably you desire to reach the goal of spending eternity with God in his great and glorious kingdom. We are presented here with the key to achieving that goal. We just need to keep walking—walking by faith. If the day you die you are still doing that, then you will "walk" straight into that city he has prepared for you. Jesus said, "My Father's house has many rooms; if that were not so, would I have told you that I am going there to prepare a place for you?" (John 14:2). The journey itself is not a cakewalk, but the final step will be an easy one. Abel, Enoch, Noah, Abraham and the other heroes of the faith we have not yet discussed all have one thing in common. Actually, they have two things in common. They admitted that they were foreigners and strangers in this world, and they did not receive the things promised, which we have now received in the new covenant. They saw them from a great distance, but we have them right in front of us. We have Jesus, his miracles, the prophecies fulfilled and the types, prefigures and foreshadows revealed in the reality found in Christ. You can do it. You can keep walking by faith.

No one said it would be easy. If you fix your eyes on things that are unseen, you will not be "normal" as far as the world is concerned. Like Abraham, you will be a foreigner and a stranger. The word translated "foreigners" is *xenoi*. This is where the English word xenophobia comes from. It means fear and hatred of foreigners—of people who are different from us. If you follow Jesus by faith, you will be different. You will not fit in. And let us face it, we all want to fit in. Sticking out in the crowd is an uncomfortable thing. Thankfully, in matters of the language we use (mostly), in the food we eat and the clothes we wear (usually), we are no different from those around us. Our difference is in the way we view the things of the world. One of the earliest church fathers said concerning the followers of Christ:

> While they [Christians] dwell in cities of Greeks and barbarians as the lot of each is cast, and follow the native customs in dress and food and other arrangements of life, yet the constitution of their own citizenship, which they set forth, is marvelous and confessedly contradicts expectation. They dwell in their own countries but only as sojourners; they bear their share in all things as citizens and they endure hardships as strangers. Every foreign country is a fatherland to them and every fatherland is foreign.... Their existence is on Earth, but their citizenship is in heaven.[14]

What the world considers important, we scoff at. Our ethic is found in the Sermon on the Mount: We think the way to greatness is through humility. We think the way to true riches lies in poverty. The way to happiness is through mourning. Are you prepared to stick out in these ways? Then you can join the club with Moses, Joshua, Noah, Jeremiah and Ruth.

The word translated as "strangers" here is *parepidemos*. Literally, it means one who "walks contrary to." It can be translated as "pilgrim" or "sojourner." As Christians we are temporary residents in this world. We walk a very different path. We are not immigrants; an immigrant seeks to join in with his or her new culture. Those who walk by the faith of Abraham definitely do not do that: "Our citizenship is in heaven" (Philippians 3:20). This world is not our home; we are just passing through. My passport may say that I (John) am a citizen of the United States of America, but it is not true, at least not in my heart. The life of a disciple is like life on a bridge. As has been said, "The world is a bridge. The wise man will pass over it but will not build his house on it." We do not put down deep roots here. You do not plant a tree on a bridge. Like Abraham, we have left our former home. We are merely temporary residents here, on the way to our true home, but we have not seen it yet. Are you ready to live your life as a sojourner? If so, then you are prepared to walk by faith.

A few years ago I was asked to have lunch with two college-age young women. I assumed that both were Christians. As we talked, I mentioned that disciples give up everything they have to follow Jesus. One of the two burst into uncontrollable tears. I was puzzled as to what I had said that made her so upset. She told me that just that week at her university she had pledged herself to "the Party." She meant the Communist Party. This was no passing commitment. She had committed herself to lifelong loyalty to the communist ideal. If she were to become a Christian, she would have to renounce her loyalty oath. She would be kicked out of the university—the thing she had dedicated all of her life toward attaining. Not only that, but with China's one-child policy, she was quite literally all that her parents lived for. If she were to become a disciple, not only would she lose everything she had lived and worked for, so would they. No wonder she was weeping. Then she looked at me and said, "I am going to do it. I am going to become a disciple of Jesus." Guess who was crying at that point. We are aliens and sojourners in this world.

Maybe you have been thinking of returning to the "country" you left when you decided to follow after Jesus. Apparently, some of those in the intended audience of Hebrews had that thought. To this, let us say, "Perish the thought!" The rest of his life, Abraham lived a few weeks' journey from his home in Mesopotamia. There was nothing preventing his return except for his decision to keep walking by faith. For us, returning to the world is easier than that. You can return to the world without even moving out of your house. But again, let us say, "Perish the thought!" Do not even think about it, because God has a better country—a heavenly one prepared for you. It is worth it. Do not stop walking by faith. If you refuse to turn back, then God will not be ashamed of you. He is proud of you and will welcome you into that city.

Believe it or not, we are only halfway through our account of the heroes of the faith. We are going to pick up the pace just a bit.

By faith Isaac blessed Jacob and Esau in regard to their future.
By faith Jacob, when he was dying, blessed each of

Joseph's sons, and worshiped as he leaned on the top of his staff.

By faith Joseph, when his end was near, spoke about the exodus of the Israelites from Egypt and gave instructions concerning the burial of his bones.

By faith Moses' parents hid him for three months after he was born, because they saw he was no ordinary child, and they were not afraid of the king's edict.

By faith Moses, when he had grown up, refused to be known as the son of Pharaoh's daughter. He chose to be mistreated along with the people of God rather than to enjoy the fleeting pleasures of sin. He regarded disgrace for the sake of Christ as of greater value than the treasures of Egypt, because he was looking ahead to his reward. By faith he left Egypt, not fearing the king's anger; he persevered because he saw him who is invisible. By faith he kept the Passover and the application of blood, so that the destroyer of the firstborn would not touch the firstborn of Israel.

By faith the people passed through the Red Sea as on dry land; but when the Egyptians tried to do so, they were drowned.

By faith the walls of Jericho fell, after the army had marched around them for seven days.

By faith the prostitute Rahab, because she welcomed the spies, was not killed with those who were disobedient. (Hebrews 11:20–31)

Joseph saw things that are invisible. His life is a picture of Jesus. He began at the right hand of his father but was sold as a slave in Egypt. Later he was raised by God to the right hand of the king of Egypt. And he saved Israel. Jesus was at the right hand of the Father, yet he came down to the earth to live as a slave among those enslaved to sin, and God raised him back up to his right hand (Philippians 2:6–9). And Jesus saved spiritual Israel— the Church. Even as he lived in the palace of Pharaoh, Joseph knew that his final resting place would be in the promised land, so he gave instructions that his bones be carried into Canaan to be buried with his father Jacob. As with the other heroes of the faith, Joseph did not receive the promises in this life, but he anticipated receiving them together with us (Hebrews

11:40). More than four hundred years later, his bones were carried by the Israelites and buried at Shechem in the promised land with his father Israel (Joshua 24:32).

Moses also "saw him who is invisible." He was living in the lap of luxury as the adopted son of Pharaoh. From the world's point of view, he had it made: he had the best food and the best clothes, and all the Egyptian princesses wanted a date with Moses. But like Jesus, he saw his people in slavery in Egypt and, also like Jesus, he left a place of comfort and safety to become like a slave so that he could free the slaves. This is what all the great heroes of the faith did. They looked at what the world has to offer and considered it all a loss compared to knowing God and to helping his people be freed from slavery. Moses saw dimly a future that we see clearly—a time when the "prophet like you from among their fellow Israelites" (Deuteronomy 18:17–18, a reference to Jesus as the second Moses) would free the captives from slavery to sin. He saw Jesus from a distance, whereas we can behold the one and only Son of God. Yet by faith he followed Jesus out of the palace, despising the fleeting pleasures of sin and considering disgrace for the sake of Christ as nothing. Why? Because he could see his reward. What palace do you need to get up out of, what fleeting pleasure do you need to walk away from, and what kind of disgrace do you need to embrace so that you can, like Moses, help put into action God's plan to free as many from slavery in Egypt as possible? Can you see the multitudes right now crossing through the Red Sea as God uses you to lead them through the waters of baptism? (Hebrews 11:29).

And consider Joshua. The Lord said to him, "See, I have delivered Jericho into your hands" (Joshua 6:2).

> *"Great, Lord, may your will be done. So, what is the battle plan?"*
>
> *"Gather the people and march around the city for six days. On the seventh day, march around it seven times."*
>
> *"Very funny, Lord; now what is the real battle plan?"*
>
> *"That is the plan. When you finish marching, blow the trumpets and the wall of the city will collapse."*

We would have liked to have been there when Joshua returned to the Israelites. "I have great news, God told me we are going to take Jericho!" "Great, what is the battle plan?" "We are going to walk around the city seven days in a row, and on the last day seven times, then we will blow the shophars and the wall will come crumbling down." "Ha, Ha! What is the real battle plan?" They must have given him an incredulous look. Yet the people literally walked by faith around that city. The people in Jericho must have thought they were crazy. Surely they shouted from the walls, "Are we supposed to be afraid of your walking around the city?" "Aren't you wearing yourself out in this blistering hot weather?" "What a bunch of fools!" They laughed at God's people because the people in Jericho were looking at the visible things. But when the horns blew and the wall fell down, they were not laughing at God's people any more. It will be the same for us if we will walk by faith around our cities or our neighborhoods.

There was one in the city of Jericho who saw with spiritual eyes. Rahab welcomed the spies despite the appearance that their cause was hopeless. God recognized her faith and saved her and her family from destruction, and to honor her faith, he caused her to be married into the line through which the Messiah came (Matthew 1:5).

There are many more heroes of the faith in the history of God's people. Our preacher wishes he had more time to tell their stories. Some we know nothing about. All of them lived by faith and saw the invisible. All saw from afar what we can see right before us.

> And what more shall I say? I do not have time to tell about Gideon, Barak, Samson and Jephthah, about David and Samuel and the prophets, who through faith conquered kingdoms, administered justice, and gained what was promised; who shut the mouths of lions, quenched the fury of the flames, and escaped the edge of the sword; whose weakness was turned to strength; and who became powerful in battle and routed foreign armies. Women received back their dead, raised to life again. There were others who were tortured, refusing to be released so that they might gain an even better resurrection. Some faced jeers and flogging, and even chains and imprisonment. They were put to death by stoning; they were sawed in two; they were killed by the sword. They went about in sheepskins and goatskins, destitute, persecuted and mistreated— the world was not worthy of them. They wandered in deserts and mountains, living in caves and in holes in the ground.
> These were all commended for their faith, yet none of them

received what had been promised, since God had planned something better for us so that only together with us would they be made perfect. (Hebrews 11:32–40)

What an awe-inspiring ending to the array of great heroes of the faith. Our narrator reaches the mountains in his dramatic recalling of the great victories God's people have achieved, not because of how much they had, but in spite of weaknesses and hardships. Surely your heart is stirred by those who sacrificed so much but received so little in this life. In their faithful vision, some achieved great victories, despite seemingly impossible odds:

- Gideon defeated Midianites "as thick as locusts" with just three hundred soldiers (Judges 7).

- Barak and Deborah defeated Sisera and the Canaanites (Judges 4–5).

- Samson singlehandedly destroyed the temple of Dagon and defeated the Philistines (Judges 16:23–31).

- Jephthah defeated the Ammonites (Judges 11–12).

God's faithful:
- Conquered kingdoms: David
- Administered justice: Samuel
- Shut the mouths of lions: Daniel
- Quenched the fury of the flames: Shadrach, Meshach and Abednego
- Escaped the edge of the sword: Elijah (1 Kings 19) and Jeremiah (Jeremiah 26)
- Women received back their dead: Elijah (1 Kings 17:17–24) and Elisha (2 Kings 4:8–37)

But not all of the faithful will experience "success" in this life. The world at that time believed that some of God's people went down to defeat. But through the eyes of faith we see a glorious future victory awaits all of them.

Some were:
- Put to death by stoning: Zechariah (2 Chronicles 24:20–22)

- Sawed in two: Isaiah (according to Jewish tradition)
- Tortured, killed by the sword, jeered at, flogged, chained, persecuted and mistreated

All of these things happened to the Jews during the time of the persecution under Antiochus Epiphanes (167–164 BC). We can read about some of the terrible tortures in the books of 1 and 2 Maccabees.[15] The Jewish Christian audience of Hebrews was well aware of this time of terrible persecution. Particularly poignant is the scene described in 2 Maccabees 7:1–41 in which Antiochus attempted to force seven brothers to eat pig flesh. When they refused, saying, "We are prepared to die rather than break the laws of our ancestors" (2 Maccabees 7:2 NJB), the king had them roasted alive, one by one, in front of their mother. When the last had perished, Antiochus killed the mother as well.

The world at that time laughed at God's people for holding on to faith in the unseen providence of God, but our Father declares, "The world was not worthy of them." The world does not deserve our sacrifice for them, but then again, we did not deserve Jesus' sacrifice for us. To those who walk by faith, God says, "You are worthy!" Don't you look forward to hearing those glorious words from your Father in heaven? "You are worthy."

All of these men and women ought to be commended by us for their faith. Actually, the best way we can commend their faith is to imitate it. None of them received what had been promised, at least not in this life. Brothers and sisters, we have all received what they only welcomed from afar. They will eventually experience salvation together with us and be made complete (v. 40), but we have salvation and perfection in this life through our high priest Jesus. We live in a state of continual forgiveness and have the Holy Spirit as a deposit, guaranteeing our salvation. Let us live worthy lives, and let us, like the heroes of old, walk by faith.

End Notes _____

12. We know from 2 Peter 2:5 that Noah preached righteousness, but the idea that he preached for 100 years is found only in Jewish tradition such as in the Sibylline Oracles and Josephus. Hopefully the reader will give us some poetic license on this claim.

13. Actually, his journey happened in two phases. First he left Ur with his father. Several years later he left all behind when he went out from Haran. Arguably, his truly faithful journey began from Haran, not from Ur. We ask you for some poetic license on this one as well!

14. From *The Letter of Diognetus*. This is a letter by an unknown author addressed to the philosopher-emperor Marcus Aurelius in about AD 150.

15. These books are included in the Old Testament Apocrypha. They can be found in the New Jerusalem Bible and the New American Bible.

Chapter 16

Look to Jesus
Hebrews 12:1–17

We now have a great picture of what it means to walk by faith. If we will, like these men and women, keep walking by faith toward the promised land, we will make it as citizens of the heavenly kingdom. We have considered the most amazing examples of faith in human history, but there is one person we have not yet talked about in our honor roll of faith. His is the greatest example of all. It is time to turn our gaze back to the pioneer and perfecter of faith, and you know who that is! He is a pioneer because he has entered the heavenly sanctuary before the rest of us. He broke into heaven and is going to wave us on in at the end of time. He has blazed the trail—leaving marks for us to follow.

But he has gone into heaven "once for all." He is not just the pioneer, he is the perfecter, the completer of our faith. He is the beginning, the middle and the end of our faith, and he is our salvation. Jesus is the one for whom the world exists, and he is also the one who exists for the world. He is eternal King and High Priest. Let us fix our eyes on him!

> *Therefore, since we are surrounded by such a great cloud of witnesses, let us throw off everything that hinders and the sin that so easily entangles. And let us run with perseverance the race marked out for us, fixing our eyes on Jesus, the pioneer and perfecter of faith. For the joy set before him he endured the cross, scorning its shame, and sat down at the right hand of the throne of God. Consider him who endured such opposition from sinners, so that you will not grow weary and lose heart.* (Hebrews 12:1–3)

After an inspiring review of the great heroes of the faith in chapter 11, we are reminded that a great cloud of witnesses is watching us and cheering us forward in our race to the finish line. If they could do it, surely we can as well. They faced more hardship than we, and they had fewer resources than we do. Of course, our spiritual race is no 100-meter dash; it is a marathon.

It is a journey, a pilgrimage that begins the moment we begin our lives in Christ. It is the growth and development of our awareness and knowledge of God, our growing understanding of Jesus, and our own spiritual maturing. Someone once said there are two great days in a person's life, the day they are born on earth and the day they realize why. Life is a great journey of discovery that everyone must take. And a "great cloud of witnesses" is cheering us on all along the way.

There is debate as to who exactly this cloud of witnesses is. The most likely explanation is that they are the heroes mentioned in chapter 11. The most extravagant theory I (Robert) have heard was that perhaps it is our friends and family in heaven or even ourselves in heaven looking back in time at our own lives. That opens up some curious possibilities.

Everyone loves to be cheered on. As parents, we know this feeling of cheering a loved one on to victory. I spent ten years of my life attending my son's soccer games every Saturday. I was his biggest fan. I loved watching him grow in skill and character as an athlete. He played at the top levels of club soccer, which challenged him to grow in physical, mental and emotional stamina. In the early days, like a pack of puppies, he and his teammates would all follow the ball around the field, and everyone tried to kick it into the goal from wherever they were on the field. Their mistakes were numerous, but as the years went by, they became better and better at being the athletes they wished to become. Sometimes it was hard, and my son wanted to quit. Sometimes he was simply tired and did not want to push ahead. We had many talks about character and mental toughness. The older he grew, the more his game depended on his own desire to be his best and on his own mental fortitude. At some point I realized he did not need my advice so much. The best I could do to help him was to cheer him on. My wife and I set out to be his biggest fans. Together, we were always excited to watch him play and root for him. This experience reminds us of Hebrews 12. We have a great cloud of witnesses rooting for us! As we live the Christian life, sometimes we need to listen to the cheers of those witnessing our race and be encouraged by them.

The word "witnesses" has multiple meanings for the hearer. In a legal setting, they are typically the ones whose testimony confirms the veracity of something. It proves a person's story as true or false. In ancient times a story had to be verified by two or more witnesses in order to be accepted as truth. The apostles were the witnesses of Jesus' miracles and of the resurrection. Early Christians were witnesses of Jesus' miraculous ministry. The word "witnesses" has another connotation. They are also the crowd of spectators watching a sporting event. The phrase "surrounded by" paints the picture of a Roman circus or a Greek theater where the crowd surrounds the participants. The hometown crowd are the cheerleaders inspiring the athletes to win the competition. Lastly, and perhaps most significantly for the audience of the book, the koine Greek word "witness" is μάρτυς, or martyr. So many of the early witnesses lost their lives for their faith that the term "witness" became synonymous with sacrificing one's life, or martyrdom. The early witnesses of Christianity are the martyrs who laid down their lives for their faith, many of whom died in Roman arenas and Greek theaters. Given the way chapter 11 ends, with the martyrdom of so many heroes in the faith, this is certainly a primary theme for us to catch in this first paragraph of chapter 12. The idea of being a martyr for the Lord is at the very core of Hebrews. Do we believe in Jesus enough that we are willing to sacrifice our lives for him?

For me, growing up in California, movies were a great part of my culture. The movie *Star Wars* defined my generation. Luke Skywalker exemplified a hero on many levels. Again and again, he put his life at risk to fight for what he believed to be right and to save his loved ones. His faith in the "good" was undaunted against all odds. Fifty years later a new Star Wars story, *Rogue One,* tells a similar tale of a band of misfits willing to die in order to defeat evil. I took all my friends from work and we watched it together, cheering on the valiant band of heroes who believed strongly enough in something to give up their lives for it. I wonder how many Christians today believe in the cause of Christ enough to do the same. This is the call of Hebrews.

Let us throw off everything that hinders...

With these things in mind, we are urged to "throw off" whatever hinders us. This is the first of a two-part command. First, we must remove anything that slows us down on our Christian path. When my son practiced soccer he used to wear weights on his ankles and a weight vest. The added weight made everything more difficult. The extra challenge made his muscles grow and his endurance level increase. In soccer as in life, much of the challenge is endurance and being able to be our best until the very end. When it came time for a real game, he took all the weights off so as not to be encumbered. He wore soccer gear, extremely light, flexible clothing made for unhindered movement. Sometimes what hinders us is not sin, which will be addressed next, but rather things that take away our focus or make us unable to live up to our decided commitment. As much as we want to, we cannot accomplish all that we wish we could. Life today is often so jam-packed with events and things to do that time becomes a major factor in deciding what we will or will not do for Christ. The "urgent" things of life come to rule our schedule. It is then that we become victims of our schedule instead of masters of it. We must be willing to cut out of our lives things that hinder our faithful walk. Sometimes the worst enemy of what is best is what is "good." Even good things can be bad, if they interfere with our pursuit of the things of the kingdom of God. What are the things you should cut out of your life that hinder your faith? For our own well-being, we are admonished to get rid of anything that hampers our walk for God.

...and the sin that so easily entangles.

Now the author addresses a core issue: sin. There are many reasons to be a Christian. Salvation is the most obvious, but the way of Christ is also the way to a great marriage, a healthy family life and good friendships. All the things that really matter in life are discovered on the trail that Jesus blazed for us. This is not to say that there are not many challenges along the route, but the way of Jesus leads us through the difficulties and the hindrances to a quality life. However, the way of Jesus is beset by many obstacles. These obstacles are sins. There is a word used in the original text, εὐπερίστατος (*euperistatos*), that is unique to the Bible. It is found nowhere else in Greek literature. It is a composite of the words "around," "easily" and "standing." In other words, it is something that is standing around us at all times that easily entangles. These sins are like traps a hunter hides all around a path. The hunted one easily steps into them, as they are everywhere, ready for the victim.

Sin is whatever lies outside of God's will for our lives. His will is that of a father for his children. A scripture often seen in Christian homes around the world is Jeremiah 29:11: "For I know the plans I have for you, declares the Lord, plans to prosper you and not to harm you, plans to give you hope and a future." Although these may be words spoken by a seventh-century-BC prophet in Jerusalem, they are recorded for us to know God's heart toward all of us. With the cultural changes we see happening in our postmodern world, the very idea of sin has become outdated. It is no longer politically correct nor culturally relevant to talk about sin. It is considered a relic of the past. Our culture is quite deceived on this point. In reality, sin is behind the explosion of divorce, the deterioration of family cohesion, the rise in depression and even the decline in health. The effects of ignoring the problem of sin are numerous and devastating.

A classic preacher's story tells of a coach who walked into the locker room and gathered all the players together. He then emptied a bag of rattlesnakes in the middle of the group. As they all screamed and leaped away for safety, he told them that was how he wanted them to treat drugs. And so it is with sin. God would have us do everything we can to stay away from sin, not because he desires to control us, but because he loves us and knows it will hinder and entangle us. Sin will keep us from effectively running the race, and it can even keep us from finishing the race altogether.

And let us run with perseverance the race marked out for us...

The idea of life being a race is a classical metaphor. Today people often say, "Life is a journey." This is the same idea. All of us have a path before us. Some of us have an easier road and others a more difficult one. Some of us are at an easier point in our lives right now, while others are at a much more difficult place. This is why we should never compare our lives to others'. Rather than looking to anyone else, we should look to Jesus and to him alone. We are told to run "with perseverance." This is a mindset necessary for success in the Christian life and essential for getting through any difficult challenge. All of us face some extremely hard times in life, and we must enter these times with our minds already set to endure and to never give up. As a young Christian, we made a decision to put our hands to the plow and never look back. We counted the cost and decided to endure whatever the world would throw at us. We did not see quitting as an option. As time has gone on, have you ever considered throwing in the towel? Probably most of us have at one time or another, despite our initial strong decision. We are about to see the cure for this problem.

...fixing our eyes on Jesus, the pioneer and perfecter of faith.

All of us have difficulty in persevering, some more than others. The solution provided to us by the writer of Hebrews is to fix our eyes on Jesus. Perhaps the greatest secret to living by faith is simply being focused on our Lord. It was when Peter took his eyes off Jesus and saw the waves that he began to sink into the water at Galilee, but when he called out to Jesus and got himself refocused, Jesus pulled him up out of danger. The experience of Peter is a great lesson for all of us. The importance of staying focused on Jesus cannot be overstated. Keeping our focus on our Savior daily reminds us continuously of the love, power and truth that supports our faith. Jesus' life is inspiring, his love is encouraging, and the power of his indestructible life is faith building. He is the *archegon* of our faith, the architect or pioneer; the trail we are trying to walk he has already walked. Everything we are attempting to do—to live a righteous life, deny sin, love others, overcome selfishness and fear, serve others and walk with faith—are all things Jesus has already done. He is the "perfecter" of our faith in that he wrestled with the many challenges and overcame doubt and temptation. He lived as the perfect example of a faithful life, even in the face of persecution and opposition. His faith grew and developed into all that God intended. Even the suffering he endured helped him become "perfect." He is not a distant and unrelatable God; he is the God who lived and walked among us, enduring everything we must endure, making him the perfect savior for us. We all struggle with temptation, and we hate to suffer. Jesus shows us the way to stay on point and never quit. Let us fix our eyes on him!

For the joy set before him he endured the cross, scorning its shame, and sat down at the right hand of the throne of God.

Keeping constantly before our mind a long-term goal is essential to overcoming short-term obstacles. It is the joy of crossing the finish line that keeps the runner running. It is the vision of victory that keeps the fighter fighting. Jesus held to the inspiration of what would follow after the pain of the cross to keep him walking to Calvary. Inspiration is incredibly important in the Christian life. Although it is full of blessings, it is also a life full of challenge. Heaven is a great motivation, and Jesus knew it was close, only a few hours or a few steps ahead. Most of us have no idea how far ahead death lies. Unfortunately, along the way we can forget about heaven. We grab on to inspiration that is nearer, such as a better marriage, a better life, freedom from sin. These are good motivators and keep us going on many a hard day. However, long-term vision is needed as well. Sometimes challenges are lengthy and slow to pass. Anyone who loses sight of the abiding blessings of an obedient life will grow weary. Over the years, it has become clear to me why I (Robert) am here. I have grown, not only in my understanding of how much God loves me, but also in my conception of how important it is that I love others. The spiritual battle has become clearer, and with it, so has my motivation. What motivates you? Consider the joy of heaven set before you. Jesus did.

Not only did Jesus consider the goal, he also scorned the shame the world threw at him. The Greek word here is also translated as "despising." Jesus did not take the shame seriously, as he considered the hearts of those who were shaming him. Philip of Neri said we should "despise the world, despise ourselves and despise the fact that we are despised." We should not allow ourselves to be overwhelmed by the scorn of those who oppose us, because the only one who matters—God—is cheering us on. If God is for us, who can be against us? "What can mere mortals do to me?" (Hebrews 13:6).

And sat down at the right hand of the throne of God.

To stand at the right hand of a king is a place of honor and respect. As we have seen, in the tabernacle the priests were allowed to stand but never to sit. This is because for one to sit in the presence of a king implies a permanent position in the throne room. Jesus certainly earned a place sitting at the right hand of God. This phrase stands in contrast to the previous one. Jesus moves from a place of utter scorn on the earth to one of immense honor in heaven. He exemplifies one of the great principles of the faith. If you are willing to be dishonored and shamed and to suffer for God here in this life, he will certainly exalt you in due time. But this requires living by faith, does it not? The picture painted of Jesus reminds us yet again of Psalm 110:1:

> *The LORD says to my lord:*
> *"Sit at my right hand*
> *until I make your enemies*
> *a footstool for your feet."*

God is the great equalizer. In the end he will set everything right. He is the God of justice, and nothing escapes his attention. There have been times in my life when I wondered "Where is God? Why hasn't he corrected this wrong, dealt with this evil person or vindicated me?" His timing is not my timing, and he certainly does not answer instantaneously to my demands. However, as time has gone by, I have seen that nobody gets away with anything. The truth always comes out in the end. Goodness and righteousness always win out. In the end, perseverance, righteousness and suffering for doing good will always be rewarded.

> *Consider him who endured such opposition from sinners, so that you will not grow weary and lose heart. In your struggle against sin, you have not yet resisted to the point of shedding your blood.* (Hebrews 12:3–4)

The writer of Hebrews challenges us. First, we are to consider Jesus and all that he went through for us. His example is inspiring and can help us to "not grow weary and lose heart." Some commentators point out that this is the phrase Aristotle used to describe runners at the end of a race who collapse and fall to the ground after crossing the finish line in victory. Other translations use the words "weak" and "faint." The idea is that we cannot give in to our weakness. There are many opportunities presented to us to give up and quit. It can be a powerful temptation.

Our world is highly averse to any form of suffering. When we first feel it, we take a pill to make it go away. In today's world suffering is eliminated as quickly as possible. Perseverance is usually developed through long-term suffering, but in our world, suffering is avoided like the plague, so perseverance is an underdeveloped character trait. Quitting is a commonly accepted solution to obstacles in our lives. Thus, many relationships do not outlast hardships. This condemns countless marriages and families. Children grow up with quitting modeled at home. Yet we cannot quit on Jesus! We cannot grow faint and bail out. We have not finished the race yet. To the Jewish Christians, the phrase "resisted to the point of shedding your blood" is a call back to the time of the Maccabees. To get a feeling for the shedding of blood that the Jews would have recalled to mind, you can read from the book of 2 Maccabees 7:1–41. William Barclay in his commentary on Hebrews points out that this was a well-known phrase from the Maccabean era. It would have both called the hearers to courage and shamed them for their lack of devotion. The Maccabees suffered and died for their faith, and we should be willing to do the same!

And have you completely forgotten this word of

encouragement that addresses you as a father addresses his son? It says,

> *"My son, do not make light of the Lord's discipline,*
> *and do not lose heart when he rebukes you,*
> *because the Lord disciplines the one he loves,*
> *and he chastens everyone he accepts as his son."*

Endure hardship as discipline; God is treating you as his children. For what children are not disciplined by their father? If you are not disciplined—and everyone undergoes discipline—then you are not legitimate, not true sons and daughters at all. Moreover, we have all had human fathers who disciplined us and we respected them for it. How much more should we submit to the Father of spirits and live! They disciplined us for a little while as they thought best; but God disciplines us for our good, in order that we may share in his holiness. No discipline seems pleasant at the time, but painful. Later on, however, it produces a harvest of righteousness and peace for those who have been trained by it.

Therefore, strengthen your feeble arms and weak knees. "Make level paths for your feet," so that the lame may not be disabled, but rather healed. (Hebrews 12:5–13)

A shift in strategy by the author points us in a new direction of thought. We are reminded that all that we suffer is actually confirmation that we are God's children. It is not a reason to grow weary and lose heart; it is a reason to be encouraged. Proverbs 3:11–12 is cited and applied to us as his "children." Context is incredibly important. A young preacher once shared a story of how his brother walked up to a car and busted the window, reached in and grabbed a woman by the blouse, and yanked her right out of the car! Was he drunk? Angry? Was this road rage? Let the context decide. It turns out that the car we are talking about was on fire from an accident. Suddenly the man changes from villain to hero. Context tells us how to feel and how to respond to an experience. Knowing that God is treating us as his children puts even suffering in the right context. Someone once asked C.S. Lewis why Christians get cancer, and he answered that it is to show the world the difference. What a great answer! Suffering with purpose is redemptive and, combined with faith, causes us to mature and become more Christlike. Suffering without faith usually makes people bitter. As someone once said to me during a difficult time, "You have a choice: get better or get bitter."

We are called to understand that God is treating us as his children. We are being disciplined! We are being treated in much the same way as any good parent treats their child. Most parents do not like disciplining their children but feel they must in order to form the right character in them. I (Robert) wish that I could have learned everything through instruction as I grew up. But in reality, there were things I only learned when I was disciplined and some only when I suffered. Raising my own children, I saw the same truth repeated often. I never wished them to have to suffer anything, but I knew that some lessons they would not accept until they had suffered the consequences of not listening. In my experience, boys often learn what they can and cannot do through suffering injury to body or ego. God blesses us in many ways, but there are certainly times that he does not make it easy. There are times when he is silent while we suffer through hardship, because he knows what it will produce in our hearts and in our character. It engenders traits vital to our long-term salvation and to being with him in heaven forever. Perseverance is necessary in order to endure the race all the way to the end. And since it is developed principally by long-term suffering, God loves us enough to leave us in tough situations so that we will make it to the finish line. The key words in this section are "sons and daughters" and "father." God gives us the context of their suffering and reminds us who we are to him: his children.

The author gives us three reasons why we should accept challenges in our lives. We should endure hardship because:

a. Those who came before you did, and they made it (Hebrews 12:1).
b. Our suffering is relatively minor compared to what Jesus endured.
c. As discipline, it is actually an expression of God's love.

What is your attitude toward the hardships that God allows to come your way? There are a few possibilities. We can:

a. Accept it with resignation
b. Accept it and get over it as soon as possible
c. Accept it but with a woe-is-me attitude
d. Accept it with resentment as punishment

e.   Accept it as coming from a loving father

It is not hard to see which is the preferred attitude that will help us make it to heaven.

> *Therefore, strengthen your feeble arms and weak knees, "Make level paths for your feet," so that the lame may not be disabled, but rather healed.*

In summary, we are called to give careful thought to what we do. We must take specific measures so that we do not fall down or grow weak. We must do whatever makes us stronger and more likely to reach the finish line. We cannot afford to be passive and merely take life as it comes. We should think carefully about the path we take and support God's efforts to make us stronger. We can make the path level by removing obstacles, and we can diligently avoid sin, which will pull us away from God. This verse is reminiscent of Proverbs 4:26: "Give careful thought to the paths for your feet and be steadfast in all your ways." Let us accept this admonition and put it into practice.

The next little section of Hebrews may seem like a small aside. It is not obviously connected with what comes before or what comes after. Perhaps it is a point that the writer of Hebrews felt was extremely important to make, but it did not fit anywhere in particular in his outline. He felt he had to say it. Why? Because our final salvation is at stake in these things. We had better not pass through this passage without pausing and looking very carefully at our lives.

> *Make every effort to live in peace with everyone and to be holy; without holiness no one will see the Lord. See to it that no one falls short of the grace of God and that no bitter root grows up to cause trouble and defile many. See that no one is sexually immoral, or is godless like Esau, who for a single meal sold his inheritance rights as the oldest son. Afterward, as you know, when he wanted to inherit this blessing, he was rejected. Even though he sought the blessing with tears, he could not change what he had done. (Hebrews 12:14–17)*

In verse 14 we see another shifting of gears. We are now heading down the mountain and moving toward wrapping up the great exhortation of the book of Hebrews. A series of exhortations are like ribbons wrapping up the gift. Be holy! Do not fall short of God's grace. Do not let bitter roots toward your fellow Christians grow in your heart. Make sure no one is sexually immoral or godless like Esau. What do all these warnings have in common? They are the things we fall into when we stop fighting the good fight. Some people visibly step away from the Lord. They stop coming to church, they stop attending gatherings, their prayer times and personal Bible study grind to a halt. It is obvious that they have left God.

Others do not stop attending, but in their hearts they have drifted away. There is no obvious change in their life except that they weaken in their convictions and give in to their sinful nature more easily. They stop living a holy life. This usually shows up in strained relationships with people from church. This person falls into bad habits, and the love of God is no longer enough to keep them on the straight and narrow path. They begin to resent the sacrifices required of the Christian life. Bitterness creeps in and replaces a once joyful, sacrificial spirit. We are warned to not be like Esau, who flippantly gave up his inheritance for a fleeting pleasure. This is the Christian who walks away for an immoral relationship, for drugs or for a lucrative career opportunity, who sells their inheritance for a cheap pleasure. One cannot walk with God and live actively in sin. Holiness is necessary to see the Lord. This is our last warning!

It seems that the concern particularly on the mind of God here is that we could be defiled by a "bitter root." This is reminiscent of Deuteronomy 29:18. In this passage, the bitter root is a remnant of idolatry in the heart, which was never sufficiently ripped out. Such bitter roots have a habit of sending out shoots and growing at our weakest point. From my experience (John), the most common cause of a bitter root in the Christian life is resentment due to being betrayed or used for selfish ends by another believer. If we are a Christian long enough, this will happen! Nothing is harder than to be mistreated by those we love. Those we love the most can also hurt us the most. This can easily lead to unresolved resentment. It is essential that we dig out these resentments by the roots so that they do not become a bitterness that defiles our hearts. Jesus tells us in the Parable of the Unmerciful Servant that if we will not forgive our brother or sister who sins against us, he will not forgive us our sins. We must pull out those roots! If we do not, we will eventually sell our soul for a pittance. Once a bitter root is allowed to grow, it is amazing what we will sell our soul for. In the case of

Esau, he sold his inheritance for a bowl of lentil stew. Insane! Impossible! But that is exactly what will happen to us if we allow resentment to grow (and Jacob gave Esau plenty of reason to let resentment grow).

What is the bitter root that might cause you to fall? You had better pull out the spiritual shovel and dig that thing out. Look at the result if you do not: "Afterward, as you know, when he wanted to inherit this blessing, he was rejected. Even though he sought the blessing with tears, he could not change what he had done." Yes, we can lose our inheritance—our salvation, and if we fall away it is irreversible. Let us take this as a solemn admonition.

Chapter 17

Summary: The Mountain of Fear and the Mountain of Joy
Hebrews 12:18-29

We have now come to the closing argument of this epic sermon. The beautiful language is loaded with emotion, and at the same time it is a summary of the line of reasoning used throughout the book.

> You have not come to a mountain that can be touched and that is burning with fire; to darkness, gloom and storm; to a trumpet blast or to such a voice speaking words that those who heard it begged that no further word be spoken to them, because they could not bear what was commanded: "If even an animal touches the mountain, it must be stoned to death." The sight was so terrifying that Moses said, "I am trembling with fear."
>
> But you have come to Mount Zion, to the city of the living God, the heavenly Jerusalem. You have come to thousands upon thousands of angels in joyful assembly, to the church of the firstborn, whose names are written in heaven. You have come to God, the Judge of all, to the spirits of the righteous made perfect, to Jesus the mediator of a new covenant, and to the sprinkled blood that speaks a better word than the blood of Abel. (Hebrews 12:18–24)

If this were a concert, here is where the singer would belt out the most dramatic crescendo. If Hebrews is a sermon, here is where the preacher would raise his voice and powerfully proclaim the truth. Our hearts would be greatly stirred. Again, as has been seen in so many places in the book of Hebrews, there is a comparison and contrast to the Hebrew past (Exodus 19:9–23; Deuteronomy 4:11, 9:8–19).

The early Hebrews escaped Egypt and came to Mount Sinai, the mountain of the Lord, to establish a new covenant. This was the holiest and most memorable event in the entire history of the Jewish people, when they received the law. There were lightening, trumpets and great winds that terrified them. The first covenant was received with great fear. The people were so afraid that they begged God to stop speaking. They remained at a distance, behind a fence. Even Moses trembled with dread. God said to Moses:

> *Put limits [a fence?] for the people around the mountain and tell them, "be careful that you do not go up the mountain or touch the foot of it. Whoever touches the mountain shall surely be put to death. He shall surely be stoned or shot with arrows; not a hand is to be laid on him. Whether man or animal, he shall not be permitted to live."* (Exodus 19:12-13)

When the first covenant was established, being in the presence of God was a thing to be avoided at all cost. If anyone crossed the barrier they were told to shoot the person with an arrow from behind the fence, and to leave the body where it lay.

Now, by contrast, we approach the new Mount Zion. The second event is nothing like the first. Instead of shaking in fear, we have angels singing and a joyful assembly! What we have in Christ is fantastically superior to anything the Jews had known. In the first covenant, coming before God inspired fear. In Christ, it inspires hope and joy. They had lightning and terrifying winds. We have thousands and thousands of angels in joyful assembly. How could they (or we) possibly consider returning to a "safe" religion based on empty ceremony and on fear? Religiosity does not give us access to the presence of God. A picture is painted of the Church and heaven and Jesus that it is welcoming and inspiring to be a part of. How could anyone resist this mountain!

Having summarized the greatness of what we have in Christ, naturally our preacher brings to an end the body of his sermon with one last admonition:

> *See to it that you do not refuse him who speaks. If they did not escape when they refused him who warned them on earth, how much less will we, if we turn away from him who warns us*

from heaven? At that time his voice shook the earth, but now he has promised, "Once more I will shake not only the earth but also the heavens." The words "once more" indicate the removing of what can be shaken—that is, created things—so that what cannot be shaken may remain.

Therefore, since we are receiving a kingdom that cannot be shaken, let us be thankful, and so worship God acceptably with reverence and awe, for our "God is a consuming fire." (Hebrews 12:25–29)

Again, a reference to the past stands in stark contrast to the present. No one who refused to listen to the voice of God on Mount Sinai escaped with their life. Yet the voice at Sinai was merely that of an angel. Now Jesus is at the right hand of God in the heavenly tabernacle, speaking from God's throne. If no one can escape who ignores the voice on earth, how much more must we pay attention to the voice from heaven? A quote from a prophecy in Haggai 2:6 reminds us that God promised he would shake things up one more time in the future. This time, not just Mount Sinai, but the whole of creation, both heaven and earth, will be shaken, leaving only God's kingdom standing. This is a more momentous event by far!

Therefore, because of all that has been said here and all that we recognize as the truth, we must be moved deeply by God. We are part of a kingdom that remains standing and unshaken. We should be thankful and worship God with awe. The original language states that we have grace and therefore should serve the Lord with reverence and holy fear. This was a powerful reminder to the Hebrew listeners who knew very well that God is holy and awesome. Jews were raised with a holy fear of God that most Gentile Christians then and now do not understand. Many Orthodox Jews will not even write the word "God." Instead they write "G¬-D." They will not say his name but rather say "the Name." The Hebrew word for worship means to prostrate oneself before God. This is a valuable lesson for us. Those of us raised Orthodox or Catholic may understand the culture of reverent fear of the Lord. Those of us who were influenced by evangelical Christianity see God more as a friend or a kind father than as a consuming fire. God is all three, of course, but it is worth noting that the Hebrew writer leaves us with a final impression of God as one to hold in reverent awe. We would do well to remember that he is a consuming fire. Our great high priest and savior Jesus Christ obeyed the Father even to death on the cross. Let us follow his great example. If we do so, we will follow him into the heavenly tabernacle to dwell with the Lord forever.

Chapter 18

Final Exhortations
Hebrews 13:1-25

In the final section of the book of Hebrews, the author changes his tone and style considerably. For all practical purposes, his sermon was completed with the dramatic summary in Hebrews 12:18–29. Now the style of the book switches to that of a personal letter, exemplified by the last few verses, which are in the form of the formal ending to a typical first-century letter. Although the formal part of his sermon is complete, our preacher is not merely throwing out a few final thoughts. The practical admonitions in chapter thirteen are central to what he is trying to accomplish in the entire sermon, and the points made are intimately connected with the message he has been delivering concerning the greatness of Jesus. This is not unlike many of Paul's letters to individual churches in which he begins with a beautiful theological treatise and follows the theology with exhortations to practical Christian living. His exhortations are intimately connected with the theology developed in the first half of his letters.

The admonitions in the last chapter of Hebrews involves discipleship, relationships in the body of Christ and worship. They are introduced with the final lines in the formal sermon: "Therefore, since we are receiving a kingdom that cannot be shaken, let us be thankful and so worship God acceptably with reverence and awe" (12:28). In chapter 13 we receive real-world advice about life in the kingdom and acceptable worship of God. The practical admonitions in this final section can be outlined as follows:

1. Brotherly love (v. 1)
2. Hospitality (v. 2)
3. Sympathy for those in troubled circumstances (v. 3)
4. Sexual purity (v. 4)
5. Contentment about the things of the world (v. 5–6)
6. Submission to godly leaders (v. 7–8, 17)
7. Confidence in the face of hostility (v. 9–14)

Let us consider the first of five of these admonitions:

Keep on loving one another as brothers and sisters. Do not forget to show hospitality to strangers, for by so doing some people have shown hospitality to angels without knowing it. Continue to remember those in prison as if you were together with them in prison, and those who are mistreated as if you yourselves were suffering.

Marriage should be honored by all, and the marriage bed kept pure, for God will judge the adulterer and all the sexually immoral. Keep your lives free from the love of money and be content with what you have, because God has said,

> *"Never will I leave you;*
>   *never will I forsake you."*
> *So we say with confidence,*
>   *"The Lord is my helper; I will not be afraid.*
> *What can mere mortals do to me?"* (Hebrews 13:1–6)

1. Brotherly Love

The first of several practical applications of what we have learned in Hebrews is this: we need to practice brotherly love. The Greek word for this kind of love is *philadelphia*, which just so happens to be the name of a famous city in the USA. It literally means the kind of love between brothers and sisters. It is family love. It is the affection felt and offered between those who know one another with great intimacy. In classic Greek this word was only applied to actual families, but the Christian church applied the word to relationships in the body of Christ. The way Peter put it, we should "love one another deeply, from the heart" (1 Peter 1:22). If we are going to make it to the promised land, we will need one another. This admonition continues a thought carried throughout the letter, as we have already been exhorted to encourage one another daily and to spur one another on to love and good deeds. Hebrews is probably not the first New Testament book that comes to mind when we think of "one another" passages, but actually it contains more than its share. Brothers and sisters, we need each other, and we need to form and build up deep, affectionate, intimate relationships. This will require that we get out of ourselves, but we need this type of love for one another, as it is a visible expression of the love God has for each of us.

2. Hospitality

Not only are we encouraged to be a true family to one another, we are admonished to extend that family atmosphere to outsiders. This would apply both to disciples of Christ whom we do not know personally and to nonbelievers. Most likely the writer of Hebrews has the former foremost in his mind here. Hospitality was a great part of the culture of the Near East in ancient times, and it still is today. However, the believers were being asked to go well beyond even what was considered the normal hospitality in the pagan culture.

The Christians in the first century were highly persecuted. It was not at all unusual for them to be forced to flee from their homes to other cities because of the persecution. Besides, a large portion of the early Church was made up of slaves, who would not be welcome in any of the homes of the pagans. In those times, the public inns were deplorable—to an extent that it would be hard for us to even imagine. Often, they were houses of ill repute. They were dirty and disease-infested, and those staying in these establishments were likely to be robbed. For this reason, the primitive Church set up an informal system of hospitality for fellow Christians. In the first century, there was obviously no phone service, and the internet was still many centuries out in the future. Refugees were likely to show up unannounced. Yet the writer of Hebrews is encouraging the believers to take them into their homes.

Those receiving the letter to the Hebrews were about to enter a period of increased pressure against their faith. Not only did they need to be willing to offer hospitality, they needed to be in a church in which they felt secure in the fact that they would be offered the same hospitality if needed. Ideally, we will get our sense of security from God, but, practically speaking, having a feeling of security from one another can help us to maintain the spiritual ideal of trusting in God alone. This security of life and home must come from within the church, so that all can step out on faith more easily.

In order to motivate the disciples, the writer of Hebrews reminds them that in some cases in the Old Testament the offer of hospitality to total strangers brought incredible blessings. He may have the story of Abraham and the three angelic visitors in Genesis 18 in mind, or perhaps his hearers are reminded of Manoah, the father of Samson in Judges 13. In both cases, the hospitality offered to strangers was well above the call of duty. Give a quick look at Genesis 18:1-15 to see. Some have taught that Hebrews 13:2 implies that we, too, might entertain angels. This seems unlikely, as the author is simply using the stories of the heroes of the faith as an inducement for us to practice hospitality, but who knows… In any case, it is time for each of us individually to ask ourselves whether we are hospitable. Do you take complete strangers into your home if asked? When was the last time you had anyone into your home? Do those who know you quite well and those with whom you are only somewhat acquainted boast about your wonderful hospitality? If you accept this admonition, then someone may very well make it to heaven because you obeyed this command. Hospitality is a major aspect of our evangelism.

3. Sympathy for Those in Trouble

When times are hard, the natural human instinct is to take care of self and family first. Christians, however, are governed by the spirit of Jesus, not by the instinct for self-preservation. Our author already mentioned in Hebrews 10:34 that the recipients of the letter of Hebrews had often helped those in prison. "You suffered along with those in prison and joyfully accepted the confiscation of your property, because you knew that you yourselves had better and lasting possessions." But notice his use of the past tense. This implies that their zeal for those in trouble had diminished considerably. When we were young Christians, we were filled with a sense of idealism. We would go anywhere and do anything for Christ. How are you doing in this area now? Have you fallen back into an attitude more like that of the world? We need to remember that those who are despised by the world are our friends. Consider the way that Jesus treated the tax collectors, prostitutes and, heaven forbid, the Samaritans. He was a friend of "sinners." Are you?

If we study the attitude of the primitive Church toward those in slavery, in prison or banished to the mines, we would be put to shame. Most of us are aware that thousands of Christians were jailed for refusing to deny their faith. What few of us know is that still more were banished to the mines. To be sent to the mines was a virtual sentence of death. At the end of the second century, the church father Tertullian wrote, "If there happen to be any in the mines or banished to the islands or shut up in prisons for nothing but fidelity to the cause of God's church, they become the nurslings of their confession." In the early second century, Ignatius had to admonish the churches against using too much of church funds to purchase the freedom of slaves. Members were irreversibly impoverishing themselves to help those in need. It is unlikely that many of us today would need to receive this admonishment. In the fourth century, in response to the work of Christians to alleviate the cruel conditions in prisons, Emperor Licinius passed a law that no one was to show kindness to sufferers in prison by supplying them with food, and that no one was to show mercy to those starving in prison.

Do we understand that it is God's desire that such help to the outcast, the illegal alien, the enslaved alcoholic and those in prison be a major part of our evangelism program? We ought to do this, not just because it can be an effective outreach, but because our high priest Jesus demonstrated for us the ministry of compassion:

> *When he saw the crowds, he had compassion on them, because they were harassed and helpless, like sheep without a shepherd. Then he said to his disciples, "The harvest is plentiful but the workers are few. Ask the Lord of the harvest, therefore, to send out workers into his harvest field."*
> (Matthew 9:36–38)

4. Sexual Purity

It may seem surprising that the writer of Hebrews would feel compelled to mention sexual purity here. Isn't it obvious that we should keep the marriage bed pure? Yes, this is obvious, but when we become weak in our faith, things that were formerly not even the slightest temptation can come into the picture. Besides, God is addressing an issue that was significant in the early Church but that is not as much a problem for us today. By the second century (and apparently as early as the first century, based on Hebrews 13:4), some were teaching that a greater righteousness could be obtained by the ascetic lifestyle. Paul allowed for the possibility of a disciple of Jesus choosing a celibate lifestyle, but some were celebrating it as a more honorable way of life than marriage and raising children in a Christian home. By way of response to this unbalanced view, these Christians are admonished that "marriage should be honored by all."

5. Contentment about Things of the World

If we fix our eyes on Jesus, not on the things of the world, then we will be content with what we have. However, by their very nature, the things of the world are visible, and the things of the kingdom of God are invisible. The temptation to take our eyes off Jesus and to look to the visible things is never-ending. That is why our author is following up an entire chapter on contentment with the things of God, not the pleasures of the world (Hebrews 11), with another reminder. As Paul put it, "Godliness with contentment is great gain" (1 Timothy 6:6). He also boldly declared, "If we have food and clothing we will be content with that" (1 Timothy 6:8).

Do you love money? Which gets more of your attention, your personal retirement plan or God's retirement plan for you? Do you really trust God in this area, or is this more a matter of words? We say, "God is in control," but then we act as if the almighty dollar or peso or euro is in control of our hearts. Aware of this temptation, the author of Hebrews reminds us of God's assurance in Deuteronomy 31:6 when he writes, "Never will I leave you; never will I forsake you." The question is whether, in the deepest part of our hearts, we actually believe this. If we do, then we will confidently declare with the psalmist, "The Lord is with me; I will not be afraid. What can mere mortals do to me?"

This is a great question for us to ask ourselves. What is the worst thing that the world can do to you? They can kill you and send you to your eternal home in heaven. Paul declared, "For to me, to live is Christ and to die is gain" (Philippians 1:21). The crazy thing is that when he said this, he really meant it! Can you join in on this chorus? If so, then you will live a life of contentment.

On a recent teaching trip I (John) found myself in Port Harcourt in Nigeria, where the problem of kidnapping of Westerners is so prevalent that I had a guard with a machine gun with me the entire time I was there. Friends asked me back in the USA, "Aren't you afraid to go there?" My answer: "The Lord is my helper; I will not be afraid. What can mere mortals do to me?" Really, what is the worst they could do to me? It would be an honor to be kidnapped for Christ. That is the least I could do for his cause. The things that produce mortal terror in the people of the world should not intimidate us if we understand the hope we have. What do you love and what do you fear?

Let us consider further admonitions from Hebrews 13:

> *Remember your leaders, who spoke the word of God to you. Consider the outcome of their way of life and imitate their faith. Jesus Christ is the same yesterday and today and forever.*
>
> *Do not be carried away by all kinds of strange teachings. It is good for our hearts to be strengthened by grace, not by*

eating ceremonial foods, which is of no benefit to those who do so. We have an altar from which those who minister at the tabernacle have no right to eat.

The high priest carries the blood of animals into the Most Holy Place as a sin offering, but the bodies are burned outside the camp. And so Jesus also suffered outside the city gate to make the people holy through his own blood. Let us, then, go to him outside the camp, bearing the disgrace he bore. For here we do not have an enduring city, but we are looking for the city that is to come.

Through Jesus, therefore, let us continually offer to God a sacrifice of praise—the fruit of lips that openly profess his name. And do not forget to do good and to share with others, for with such sacrifices God is pleased.

Have confidence in your leaders and submit to their authority, because they keep watch over you as those who must give an account. Do this so that their work will be a joy, not a burden, for that would be of no benefit to you. (Hebrews 13:7–17)

We are going to glean two more admonitions from this section.

6. Submission to Godly Leaders

The principle motivation for us to hold on to our faith should be our hope in Jesus. However, the writer of Hebrews knows that we sometimes need the help of a living, breathing example to bolster the faith we put in Christ. For example, when we are tempted to waver in our faith, we can remind ourselves that Jesus is not the only one who has fought the good fight, has finished the race and kept the faith (paraphrasing 2 Timothy 4:7). In a sense, he is not the only pioneer for us. When we are tempted to get caught up in the stuff the world throws at us and to lose our focus on doing what is right, we can look to Jesus for an example, but we can also consider the outcome of the exemplary lives of faithful disciples we have known. We are to put our faith in the unseen, but a positive, visible example can sometimes help. We all know of brothers and sisters who have faithfully exemplified Christian ideals. We also have known others who have fallen short of the ideal. We can "consider the outcome of their way of life." What was the result of their lives? Who was more blessed by God in the end? Whose faith had we best imitate? Was it worth it for them to give up everything for Christ? We know it was, as experience tells us so. What was said at their funeral? What do you want said at yours?

"Jesus Christ is the same yesterday and today and forever." In other words, if he was faithful to those who came before you, he will be faithful to you as well. We can rest assured of this. It will be worth it!

We will skip down to Hebrews 13:16–17, where our author finishes his thoughts about our relationship with those who lead the Church. God is exhorting us to willingly put ourselves under the authority of those who lead us. Theirs is an authority delegated to them by God; therefore, they will give an account. Many biblical examples inform us that God's people do best when there is a godly man leading them. We all want to be part of a group that is going somewhere, do we not? If our local ministry is stuck and directionless, this can only hurt our own faith. However, the leaders cannot very well lead the Church anywhere if the members will not follow them. The godly leader is the servant of all, and he or she does not lord it over the flock. Therefore, for the Church to work as a unit, the members must freely offer themselves to submit to the leaders. Like Deborah said, "When the princes in Israel take the lead, when the people willingly offer themselves— praise the Lord!" (Judges 5:2). Does this mean that the members will always agree with the direction taken? Obviously not, but if the leader has to cajole or beg the members to support the course they have set, that would make their work a burden, not a joy. Eventually, they will become burned out and will stop courageously leading the Church.

Who is hurt the most if we will not support our leaders? We are, "for that would be of no benefit to [us]." If we drag our feet rather than support a program of the church, we might as well shoot ourselves in the foot. Let us support our leaders in the name of Christ.

7. Confidence in the Face of Hostility

It is a bit difficult to understand exactly where our author is trying to take us in Hebrews 13:9–14. He begins by encouraging us to find our spiritual strength from the grace of God rather than in religious ceremony. It is not clear what "strange teachings" he is talking about, but most likely they were coming from Judaizers—those who were encouraging the Christians to rely on Jewish forms of worship for righteousness. We are well aware that the hearers of this sermon were strongly tempted to return to these forms of worship so that they could avoid persecution. They were tempted to rely on sacrifices at the altar in the old and fading ceremonies of Judaism. But we have a far greater tabernacle, do we not? We have Jesus, the author and perfecter of a much greater salvation.

Although we no longer observe the sacrifices in the law of Moses, the Hebrew writer draws an example from the sin offering to help us think about how we should deal with those who oppose us. False teachers will mock us and may even try to put us out of their churches, but, just as the sin offering is burned outside the camp, Jesus was killed outside the gate of Jerusalem, at Golgotha. As he has reminded us repeatedly throughout the letter, our preacher is urging us to look to Jesus when we are opposed: "Let us, then, go to him outside the camp, bearing the disgrace he bore." It is far better to bear disgrace for the sake of Christ than to compromise our conviction, be it with the world or even with those within the Church who are not being faithful to the gospel. We need to be reminded that in this world there is no enduring city, "but we are looking for the city that is to come." Many will try to base their Christianity on human rules. Others will slip back into being religious rather than Christlike. They may not appreciate it when we set the example of true sacrificial Christian living. They may even oppose us because our example makes them look bad. The honest truth is that this can be really hard, because all of us want to be liked. However, being Christlike does not always make one popular. What should we do? We should go to Christ, outside the camp, if necessary bearing the disgrace he bore, for we are putting our hope in the eternal city, which is to come.

Hebrews 13:15–16 is our author's summary of this section. In all these things, whether in our relationships with one another, whether we are serving those inside or outside the Church, whether we are resisting temptation, refusing ourselves the pleasures of the world or experiencing opposition, even in the Church, the key is for us to offer praise to God. This "sacrifice of praise" is probably a reference to the fellowship offering, which is described in Leviticus 7:11–15. The fellowship offering was given "as an expression of thankfulness." In Romans 15:16 we are reminded of "the priestly duty of proclaiming the gospel of God, so that the Gentiles might become an offering acceptable to God, sanctified by the Holy Spirit." Thanks to our high priest Jesus, we no longer need to make sacrifices for sin. Amen for that, but we can and we should continue to make sweet-smelling offerings to God by doing good and sharing with others, "for with such sacrifices God is pleased."

The last little section of Hebrews is the most intimate in the book. It is a personal note between the author and his close brothers and sisters in the faith.

> *Pray for us. We are sure that we have a clear conscience and desire to live honorably in every way. I particularly urge you to pray so that I may be restored to you soon.*
>
> *Now may the God of peace, who through the blood of the eternal covenant brought back from the dead our Lord Jesus, that great Shepherd of the sheep, equip you with everything good for doing his will, and may he work in us what is pleasing to him, through Jesus Christ, to whom be glory for ever and ever. Amen.*
>
> *Brothers and sisters, I urge you to bear with my word of exhortation, for in fact I have written to you quite briefly.*
>
> *I want you to know that our brother Timothy has been released. If he arrives soon, I will come with him to see you.*
>
> *Greet all your leaders and all the Lord's people. Those from Italy send you their greetings.*
>
> *Grace be with you all.* (Hebrews 13:18–25)

From this section we learn that the writer of the letter is personally acquainted with those to whom he is writing. As a friend, he is asking them to pray for him, particularly that he will be able to visit them soon. He then appends to the letter a formal ending, which scholars call a benediction—an invocation of divine blessing on them. One last time he reminds them to consider Jesus, the great Shepherd and God who will equip them for doing his will. He then includes a private postscript letting them know that Timothy, most likely Paul's companion in the faith, has been freed and will hopefully come to visit those to whom the letter was addressed.

We hope that you, too, have been able to bear with our word of exhortation, although we are not so sure we can call it brief! Our intent has been that of the Hebrew writer, which is that you may be encouraged in your faith. Brothers and sisters, let us fix our eyes on Jesus, the beginning, middle and end of our faith. You can do it. You will make it if you will take these exhortations to heart. God has a city prepared for you. If we will keep walking by faith, put on spiritual blinders to the things of the world and keep our eyes fixed on Jesus, we will all walk together on that heavenly road to that heavenly city, right into the waiting arms of our Lord and Savior Jesus Christ.

Books for Christian Growth from Illumination Publishers

Apologetics

Compelling Evidence for God and the Bible—Truth in an Age of Doubt, by Douglas Jacoby.

Field Manual for Christian Apologetics, by John M. Oakes.

Is There A God—Questions and Answers about Science and the Bible, by John M. Oakes.

Mormonism—What Do the Evidence and Testimony Reveal?, by John M. Oakes.

Reasons For Belief–A Handbook of Christian Evidence, by John M. Oakes.

That You May Believe—Reflections on Science and Jesus, by John Oakes/David Eastman.

The Resurrection: A Historical Analysis, by C. Foster Stanback.

When God Is Silent—The Problem of Human Suffering, by Douglas Jacoby.

Bible Basics

A Disciple's Handbook—Third Edition, Tom A. Jones, Editor.

A Quick Overview of the Bible, by Douglas Jacoby.

Be Still, My Soul—A Practical Guide to a Deeper Relationship with God, by Sam Laing.

From Shadow to Reality—Relationship of the Old & New Testament, by John M. Oakes.

Getting the Most from the Bible, Second Edition, by G. Steve Kinnard.

Letters to New Disciples—Practical Advice for New Followers of Jesus, by Tom A. Jones.

The Baptized Life—The Lifelong Meaning of Immersion into Christ, by Tom A. Jones.

The Lion Never Sleeps—Preparing Those You Love for Satans Attacks, by Mike Taliaferro.

The New Christian's Field Guide, Joseph Dindinger, Editor.

Thirty Days at the Foot of the Cross, Tom and Sheila Jones, Editors.

Christian Living

According to Your Faith—The Awesome Power of Belief in God, by Richard Alawaye.

But What About Your Anger—A Biblical Guide to Managing Your Anger, by Lee Boger.

Caring Beyond the Margins—Understanding Homosexuality, by Guy Hammond.

Golden Rule Membership—What God Expects of Every Disciple, by John M. Oakes.

How to Defeat Temptation in Under 60 Seconds, by Guy Hammond.

Jesus and the Poor—Embracing the Ministry of Jesus, by G. Steve Kinnard.

How to Be a Missionary in Your Hometown, by Joel Nagel.

Like a Tree Planted by Streams of Water—Personal Spiritual Growth, G. Steve Kinnard.

Love One Another—Importance & Power of Christian Relationships, by Gordon Ferguson.

One Another—Transformational Relationships, by Tom A. Jones and Steve Brown.

Prepared to Answer—Restoring Truth in An Age of Relativism, by Gordon Ferguson.

Repentance—A Cosmic Shift of Mind & Heart, by Edward J. Anton.

Strong in the Grace—Reclaiming the Heart of the Gospel, by Tom A. Jones.

The Guilty Soul's Guide to Grace—Freedom in Christ, by Sam Laing.

The Power of Discipling, by Gordon Ferguson.

The Prideful Soul's Guide to Humility, by Tom A. Jones and Michael Fontenot.

The Way of the Heart—Spiritual Living in a Legalistic World, by G. Steve Kinnard.

The Way of the Heart of Jesus—Prayer, Fasting, Bible Study, by G. Steve Kinnard.

Till the Nets Are Full—An Evangelism Handbook for the 21st Century, by Douglas Jacoby.

Walking the Way of the Heart—Lessons for Spiritual Living, by G. Steve Kinnard.

When God is Silent—The Problem of Human Suffering, by Douglas Jacoby.

Values and Habits of Spiritual Growth, by Bryan Gray.

Deeper Study

A Women's Ministry Handbook, by Jennifer Lambert and Kay McKean.

After The Storm—Hope & Healing From Ezra—Nehemiah, by Rolan Dia Monje.

Aliens and Strangers—The Life and Letters of Peter, by Brett Kreider.

Crossing the Line: Culture, Race, and Kingdom, by Michael Burns.

Daniel—Prophet to the Nations, by John M. Oakes.

Exodus—Making Israel's Journey Your Own, by Rolan Dia Monje.

Exodus—Night of Redemption, by Douglas Jacoby.

Finish Strong—The Message of Haggai, Zechariah, and Malachi, by Rolan Dia Monje.

Free Your Mind—40 Days to Greater Peace, Hope, and Joy, by Sam Laing.

In Remembrance of Me—Understanding the Lord's Supper, by Andrew C. Fleming.

In the Middle of It!—Tools to Help Preteen and Young Teens, by Jeff Rorabaugh.

Into the Psalms—Verses for the Heart, Music for the Soul, by Rolan Dia Monje.

King Jesus—A Survey of the Life of Jesus the Messiah, by G. Steve Kinnard.

Jesus Unequaled—An Exposition of Colossians, by G. Steve Kinnard.

Mornings in Matthew, by Tammy Fleming.

Passport to the Land of Enough—Revised Edition, by Joel Nagel.

Prophets I—The Voices of Yahweh, by G. Steve Kinnard.

Prophets II—The Prophets of the Assyrian Period, by G. Steve Kinnard.

Prophets III—The Prophets of the Babylonian and Persion Periods, by G. Steve Kinnard.

Return to Sender—When There's Nowhere Left to God but Home, by Guy Hammond.

Romans—The Heart Set Free, by Gordon Ferguson.

Revelation Revealed—Keys to Unlocking the Mysteries of Revelation, by Gordon Ferguson.

Spiritual Leadership for Women, Jeanie Shaw, Editor.

The Call of the Wise—An Introduction and Index of Proverbs, by G. Steve Kinnard.

The Cross of the Savior—From the Perspective of Jesus..., by Mark Templer.

The Final Act—A Biblical Look at End-Time Prophecy, by G. Steve Kinnard.

The Gospel of Matthew—The Crowning of the King, by G. Steve Kinnard.

The Letters of James, Peter, John, Jude—Life to the Full, by Douglas Jacoby.

The Lion Has Roared—An Exposition of Amos, by Douglas Jacoby.

The Seven People Who Help You to Heaven, by Sam Laing.

The Spirit—Presense & Power, Sense & Nonsense, by Douglas Jacoby.

Thrive—Using Psalms to Help You Flourish, by Douglas Jacoby.

What Happens After We Die?, by Douglas Jacoby.

World Changers—The History of the Church in the Book of Acts, by Gordon Ferguson.

Marriage and Family

A Lifetime of Love—Building and Growing Your Marriage, by Al and Gloria Baird

Building Emotional Intimacy in Your Marriage, by Jeff and Florence Schachinger.

Hot and Holy—God's Plan for Exciting Sexual Intimacy in Marriage, by Sam Laing.

Faith and Finances, by Patrick Blair.

Friends & Lovers—Marriage as God Designed It, by Sam and Geri Laing.

Mighty Man of God—A Return to the Glory of Manhood, by Sam Laing.

Pure the Journey—A Radical Journey to a Pure Heart, by David and Robin Weidner.

Raising Awesome Kids—Being the Great Influence in Your Kids' Lives by Sam and Geri Laing..

Principle-Centered Parenting, by Douglas and Vicki Jacoby.

The Essential 8 Principles of a Growing Christian Marriage, by Sam and Geri Laing.

The Essential 8 Principles of a Strong Family, by Sam and Geri Laing.

Warrior—A Call to Every Man Everywhere, by Sam Laing.

All these and more available at www.ipibooks.com

www.EvidenceForChristianity.org